'Keiri Zaimu' saves the world

Introduction to Japanese ACCOUNTING AND FINANCE Practices

Comprehensive Manual for Accountants and CFOs

Akira Kaneko Tadashi Ishida Ryuji Aoyama
Kazunori Baba Shinsuke Okuaki Miwako Noda

経済産業省
経理・財務人材育成事業

税務経理協会
Zeimu Keiri Kyokai

Copyright © 2017 by Akira Kaneko, Tadashi Ishida, Ryuji Aoyama, Kazunori Baba, Shinsuke Okuaki, Miwako Noda,. All rights reserved.
Published by Zeimu Keiri Kyokai Co.,Ltd., Tokyo. Japan

Translated by Naoya Sakamoto (CPA), Geraldine S. Batoon (CIA) from iCube, Inc., and reviewed by Masashi Jodai (USCPA) of Furukawa Electric Co.,Ltd. and four members from Nifco Inc. and its subsidiaries, Tsutomu Mannari, John Dieker, Doug Binks and T. Jeerawat. (from Japanese into English)

No part of this publication may be reproduced, stored in a retrieval system, or transmitted in any form or by any means, electronic, mechanical, photocopying, recording, scanning, or otherwise, without the prior written permission of the publisher. Requests to the Publisher for permission should be addressed to the Permission Department, Zeimu Keiri Kyokai Co.,Ltd., 2-5-13 Shimoochiai Shinjuku-ku, Tokyo, Japan 161-0033, Tel:81-3-3953-3301, Fax:81-3-3565-3391, e-mail:info@zeikei.co.jp, http://www.zeikei.co.jp

The publication is designed to provide accurate and authoritative information in regard to the subject matter covered. It is sold with the understanding that the publisher and authors are not engaged in rendering legal, accounting, or other professional services. If professional advice or other expert assistance is required, the services of a competent professional person should be sought.

ISBN 978-4-419-06503-4
Printed in Japan

Upon publication of the English version of
Introduction to Japanese "Accounting and Finance" Practices
— A tribute to late Mr. Akira Kaneko, a bellwether of Japanese-style CFOs —

I am very pleased to learn that *Introduction to Japanese "Accounting and Finance" Practices* will be translated and published in English.

It is five years since the first edition of the book in Japanese was published in April 2012. We originally published it as a practical manual for all finance & accounting professionals in response to a fervent request from late Mr. Akira Kaneko, who had served as a CFO of Shin-Etsu Chemical Co., Ltd., a Japanese public company that has sustained high profitability for a long time.

As the book was initially intended to be used by accountants who belong to accounting & finance departments of Japanese companies, it was written from a practical viewpoint by professionals not only qualified as registered tax accountant or certified public accountant but also equipped with vast knowledge and experience acquired through their day-to-day practice.

While you can find numerous accounting & finance publications in Japan and across the world, many of them are academic books for accounting researchers or preparation books for CPA exam. In fact, there only few books that are truly written for practitioners.

As those of you who have chosen this book may be well aware, the convergence of accounting standards is a global trend. Accordingly, we can say that the concept or technical terminology used in the field of accounting & finance is now common throughout the world no matter whether it is expressed in Japanese words or English words.

As an editor, I would be more than delighted if you would make this English version a desktop companion that helps you perform your job as a corporate financial accountant and would realize that there is indeed no border in the world of accounting & finance.

July 2017
Tadashi Ishida, CPA (Japan) and Editor

「経理・財務マニュアル」英語版発刊にあたって
──日本のCFOの先導者であった故金児昭さんへ──

　今回、『キャリアアップを目指す人のための「経理・財務」実務マニュアル』が英語版で発刊されるのを大変に喜んでいます。
　2012年4月に初版が刊行されて5年が経過しました。
　もともとこの本は日本の上場企業で長い間、高収益を維持している信越化学工業株式会社のCFOであった故金児昭さんからの強い要望で、「すべての経理・財務パーソンに読んでいただける実務書」として刊行されました。
　発刊当初は日本企業の経理・財務部門に所属するAccountantsを対象に実務的な観点から書かれました。従って執筆者は税理士、公認会計士の資格を有するだけでなく、日々の実務を通して培った豊富な知識と事例を持ち合わせている人たちです。

　ご承知のとおり経理・財務の専門書は日本だけでなく世界各国で出版されています。但し、その多くは会計学の研究者を対象とした学術書であったり、公認会計士試験の受験参考書であったりして、真に実務家を対象にしたものは少ないのです。
　この本を手に取る皆さんはお分かりだと思いますが、「会計は最終的に一箇所に収斂する」という言葉があるとおり、経理・財務の分野は日本語であれ英語であれ、その考え方や使用する用語（Technical Terminology）に使う言語は違っても世界共通です。

　是非この英語版を皆さんの机の上においていただき、企業のFinancial Accountantとして実務に役立てるだけでなく、「経理・財務の世界に国境はない」ことを確認して頂ければ編集者としてこれに勝る喜びはありません。

2017年7月
編集者：石田正
公認会計士（日本）

Foreword

Akira Kaneko was a well-known leader in Japan's Finance and Accounting world. After entering Shin-Etsu Chemical, the large chemical company in Japan, in 1961, he gained experience throughout his career in the Finance and Accounting organizations. He went on to be named CFO in 1992, a post which he held until 1999, while concurrently making significant public contributions as a member of the Certified Public Accountant Examination Committee (responsible for writing and oral examinations) and also as an advisor to the Financial Supervisory Agency (specialized in Corporate Accounting).

Additionally, he published over 100 books and was truly a pioneer as a Japanese CFO passionate about Finance and Accounting instruction. Passing away in the winter of 2013, he was mourned by all.

For the book *Introduction to Japanese "Accounting and Finance" Practices*, which inspired this book, Kaneko acted as the supervising editor overseeing the writing edited by Tadashi Ishida (CPA), and completed by us, a team of a CPA and tax accountants. During the process of writing and publishing of this book, we had many opportunities to consult with Kaneko; he always emphasized, "Although Accounting and Finance organizations must insist on ethical and fair practices and may be disliked for doing so, we also must get to know people, support other functions, and do our best to bring others happiness. 'Japanese style Accounting and Finance' (Keiri Zaimu) is precisely the method to achieve those goals." We also agreed strongly with these sentiments.

Following that project, the Executive Director of Japan Association for CFOs Hiroshi Yaguchi and the Executive Managing Director of Zeimu Keiri Kyokai Co.,Ltd Katsuyuki Otsubo (currently President and CEO), who had been closely involved with several of Kaneko's books, shared that he wanted to continue Kaneko's legacy in spreading "Japanese style Accounting and Finance" (Keiri Zaimu) to the world. And so, this book was planned, and following two years of effort that vision is finally coming to fruition.

This book is written to explain the workings of Japanese systems of Accounting and Finance, to aid in the actual day to day operations of people working in the Finance organizations in overseas branches of Japanese companies. In the original version, this book is divided into the major sections of 1. Business Operations, 2.

Main Points in Accounting, 3. Main Points in Tax, and finally 4. Internal Controls. However, the perspective for sections 2 and 3 is specific to Japan only, and so is not included in the English version, which is edited to focus on 1. Business Operations and 4. Internal Controls.

This is because although accounting standards and tax regulations vary by country, business operations and internal controls can be said to have many similarities even across countries; therefore, we are confident that sharing the essence of "Japanese style Accounting and Finance" meets the goal to share Japan's best practices.

The publishing of this book would not have been possible without the efforts of Naoya Sakamoto (CPA), Geraldine S. Batoon (CIA), Masashi Jodai (USCPA) of Furukawa Electric Co., Ltd. And four members from Nifco Inc. and its subsidiaries, Tsutomu Mannari, John Dieker, Doug Binks and T. Jeerawat for their input and contributions to the English translation from the stance of their professional expertise. Deep gratitude for your assistance in this project.

2017 Authors
Ryuji Aoyama
Kazunori Baba
Shinsuke Okuaki
Miwako Noda

まえがき

　日本には、経理・財務の実務界に、金児昭という著名な指導者がおられました。金児先生は、1961年に日本の優良化学メーカーである信越化学工業株式会社に入社後、一貫して経理、財務部門でキャリアを重ね、1992年に同社の常務取締役（CFO）に就任され、1999年まで務められる一方で、公認会計士試験（筆記・口述）試験委員や金融監督庁顧問（企業会計担当）等公職でもすばらしい実績を残されました。

　また、多忙な中100冊を超える書籍を出版されるなど、経理・財務教育に情熱を傾けられた日本のCFOの先導者でありましたが、2013年冬に永眠され、皆から惜しまれました。

　この書籍のもととなった『キャリアアップを目指す人のための「経理・財務」実務マニュアル』は、金児先生が監修し、石田正先生の編集の下、私たち公認会計士・税理士が執筆を担当したものです。この書籍を出版する過程で、金児先生とたびたび打ち合わせをする機会がありましたが、金児先生はたえず、「経理・財務部門は、公正を貫き時には憎まれ役にもなりながらも、人を知り、他部門に仕え、人を幸せにするように努めなければならないのです。そして、「日本型経理・財務」こそ、それを実現できる手段なのです。」と語ってこられ、我々も大変共感したものでした。

　その後、日本CFO協会（JACFO）の谷口宏専務理事と金児先生の書籍を数多く手がけられてきた税務経理協会の大坪克行常務取締役（現、代表取締役社長）から、是非とも金児先生の遺志を引き継ぎ、「日本版経理・財務」を世界に広げていきたい、と本書が企画され、2年の月日が流れ、ようやく日の目をみることとなりました。

　本書は、日系企業の海外子会社の経理部門にお勤めの方に、実務に役立つよう、日本の経理・財務制度を解説した書籍です。元の書籍では、大きく1.業務プロセス、2.会計上のポイント、3.税務上のポイント及び4.内部統制上のポイントの4つの視点から解説をしていますが、2.会計上のポイント、3.税務上のポイントの視点は日本特有の要件となっていることから英語版では省略し、1.業務プロセス及び4.内部統制上のポイントに絞って編集しています。

　なぜなら、会計基準や税法は国が違えば様々ですが、業務プロセスや内部統制はある程度国が違っても共通部分が多いうえ、日本のベストプラクティスをお伝えす

ることが「日本版経理・財務」の核心を伝えることになると確信しているからです。したがって、本書を読んで「日本版経理・財務」のコアをマスターしていただけますと幸いです。

　なお、本書の刊行にあたっては、プロフェッショナルの見地から英訳作業に多大な貢献をしていただきました坂本直弥（Naoya Sakamoto）さん（CPA）、Geraldine S. Batoon（CIA）さん、古河電気工業株式会社の上代昌史（Masashi Jodai）さん（USCPA）、株式会社ニフコとその子会社から萬成力（Tsutomu Mannari）さん、John Dieker さん、Doug Binks さん、ジーラワットさん（T. Jeerawat）の尽力なくしては実現がなかったと思います。この場をお借りして厚く御礼申し上げます。

2017年　執筆者一同
青山　隆治
馬場　一徳
奥秋　慎祐
野田美和子

Contents

1. Accounts Receivable Management 1

Process Flow 1
1. Credit Management to Settlement 1
2. Receivable Management by Customer 5
3. Sales Discount and Rebate 7

Accounting Key Points 7
1. Recognition 7
2. Evaluation 8
3. Journal Entries 9

Internal Control Key Points 11
1. Credit Management 11
2. Contact (Order Taking) 11
3. Posting of Sales 11
4. Billing/Invoicing 11
5. Settlement 12
6. Receivable Management by Customer 12
7. Treatment of Delinquent Receivables/Doubtful Accounts 12
8. Treatment of Sales Allowance and Rebates 12

2. Accounts Payable Management 14

Process Flow 14
1. Supplier Management 14
2. Purchase Contract 15
3. Purchase 16
4. Monitoring and Settlement/Payment 17
5. Purchase Returns and Allowances/Purchase Discount 18

Accounting Key Points 19
1. Recognition 19
2. Cost of Purchase 20
3. Special Types of Purchases 20
4. Journal Entries 21

Internal Control Key Points 22
1. Inspection 22
2. Settlement - (Segregation of Duties) 22
3. Management of Payable Balance - (By Statement Reconciliations) 22
4. Investigation on Outstanding Accounts Payable 23

3. Inventory Management 24

Process Flow 24
1. Balance Management 24
2. Management of Inventory/Stock Receipt and Inventory/Stock Issuance 27
3. Maintaining Proper Inventory Level 28

Accounting Key Points 30
1. Scope of Inventories 30
2. Cost of Inventories 31
3. Measurement of Inventories 32

Internal Control Key Points 33
1. Balance Management 33
2. Verification of Inventory/Stock Issues and Inventory/Stock Receiving 34
3. Proper Inventory Level Management 35

4. Fixed Asset Management 37

Process flow 38
1. Acquisition of Fixed Asset 38
2. Management and Maintenance of Fixed Asset 39
3. Disposal of Fixed Assets 40

Internal Control Key Points 40
1. Estimated Risks 40
2. Internal Control Key Points 41

5. Software Management 43
Process Flow 44
1. Confirming Purpose of Software Production
   (at the time of planning of software production) 44
2. Ledger Management 44
3. Depreciation 44

Internal Control Key points 45
1. Internally-Used/Developed Software 45
2. Software for the Purpose of Market Sales
   (Packaged Software) 46

6. Cost Management 47
Process Flow 47
1. Cost Budgeting 47
2. Actual Cost Calculation 48
3. Computation/Calculation by Product 49
4. Cost Variance Analysis 49

Internal Control Key Points 49
1. Defining the Authority and Responsibility in Manufacturing Operation 49
2. Appropriateness of Estimated Items 50
3. Validity of Aggregation Procedures 50

7. Expense Management 51
Process Flow 51
1. Budget 51
2. Expense Processing 51
3. Settlement/Payment 52

Internal Control Key Points 52
1. Payroll Expenses 52
2. Operating Expenses 53

8. Monthly Performance Management 55
Process Flow 56
1. Monthly Closing Adjustment 56

    2. Monthly Performance Verification 57
    3. Budget Review 58

9. Financial Closing Process 60
Process Flow 60
    1. Preparations in Advance 60
    2. Financial Closing Procedures 62
    3. Reporting to Directors and Preparation of Audit 66
    4. Preparation for the General Meeting of Shareholders
       (In Case of Japan) 68
Internal Control Key Points 69

10. Annual Budget Management 72
Process Flow 72
    1. Developing Budget Management Policy 72
    2. Developing Budget by Department 73
    3. Finalizing Annual Budget 73
Budget Management Key Points 74
    1. Significance of Budgeting 74
    2. Work Flow of Budgeting 75
    3. Setting Method 75
    4. Responsibility of Budgeting 76
    5. Budget Period 77
    6. Unit of Budget 77
    7. Relationship with the Medium and Long-term Planning 77
    8. System of Budget 77
    9. Selling Budget 78
    10. Production Budget 79
    11. General Administrative Expenses Budget 81
    12. Non-Operating Profit and Loss Budget 81
    13. Investment/Capital Budget 82
    14. Fund Budget 82
    15. Overall Budget 83
    16. Review of Budget 83

17. Progress Management of Budget	84
18. Analysis of Variance between Budget and Actual Results	85

11. Cash and Bank Control 88
Process Flow 88
1. Bank Deposits and Withdrawals 88
2. Petty Cash Fund Control 91
3. Cash and Deposit Balance Control 93

Internal Control Key Points 95
1. Control Environment 95
2. Risk Assessment 96
3. Control Activities 97
4. Information and Communication 97
5. Monitoring 97
6. Information and Communication 98

12. Loan Payable Management 99
1. Types of Loan 101
2. Types of Financial Institutions 103

Process Flow 104
1. Loan Execution 105
2. Loan Management 107

Internal Control Key Points 109
1. Control Environment 109
2. Risk Assessment 109
3. Control Activities 110
4. Information and Communication 110
5. Monitoring 110
6. Information Technology 110

13. Foreign Exchange (FOREX) Management 112
1. What is Foreign Exchange? 112
2. Foreign Exchange Market 112
3. Exchange Rate 113

  4. Exchange Risk and Hedging Method 113
 Process Flow 116
  1. FOREX Management 116
  2. Term-End Evaluation 118
  3. Foreign Currency Deposit Management 119

14. Fund Management 120
 Process Flow 120
  1. Medium-Term and Long-Term Fund Management 120
  2. Annual Fund Management 121

Index 128

1. Accounts Receivable Management

Sales are not only about selling products. It is only completed when the payment is collected. Collection is very important for the company's cash flow. If the management fails to collect, cash shortage can occur and it will eventually impact the operations. The worst case scenario is that there will be no available cash for purchases and the payment of expenses.

This chapter explores topics on practical accounts receivable management related to sales.

Process Flow

1. Credit Management to Settlement

| Credit Management | Contract (Order Taking) | Posting of Sales | Billing | Settlement |

(1) Credit Management

Credit Management is a risk management process that sets the company's criteria for approved customers and clients. The criteria should include the credit ceiling for each customer and periodic assessments for adjustment based on current situations.

The company should judge using both quantitative factors like financial analysis and qualitative factors like visiting customers.

A. New Customers

When the company conducts business with a new customer, the Management or the Credit Department should set a credit limit based on the result of the credit investigation. Such investigations should include using established credit agencies as guide plus an understanding of the customers international corporate structure to establish credit risk in each country the customer operates (a customer's subsidiary may not be credit worthy when not backed by parental guarantees). It is necessary to remind the Sales Department to ensure compliance with the corporate credit policy.

Setting up of the Customer Master List

Management should set up a Customer Master List based on approved contracts and approved credit limits. Good practices include setting up a credit limit that is based on authorized criteria. The credit limit should be in compliance with the company policy and authorized by the management.

B. Existing Customers

A periodic review of existing customer's financial statements should be performed. Short-term capacity to pay (liquidity), long term capacity to pay (solvency), appropriateness of credit limit, and paying habits are perspectives that can be used when reviewing the customer.

[Establishing New Credit Limits]

```
                                    Examining         Examining
                                    Commercial        employee
                                    registry          turnover rate

                                    Examining         Examining
                                    correspondent     executives
                                    financial         background
                                    institutions
                        Collecting                    Examining
                        industry                      capital
                        information  Interviewing     structure
                                     concerned
                                     divisions                    Referring
                                                                  in-house
Arranging                            Visiting        Verifying    credit criteria
requests for  Collecting             customers       qualitative
credit check  credit reports                         areas        Performing     Making a
                                     Collecting                   overall        decision on    Establishing   Approval of
                                     rating data                  evaluation of  the transaction credit limits  credit limits
                        Collecting               Performing       analysis results
                        financial data           a financial
                                                 analysis                Examining
              Collecting                                                 customers
              financial             Examining     Examining              growth
              statements            normal working accounts              potential
                          Collecting capital       payable
                          information              turnover             Examining
              Collecting  on sales trends                               customers
              information on          Examining trends  Calculating     relationship
              borrowing               in operating      inventory
                          Collecting  margins           turnover        Evaluating
                          clearing                                      amount
                          conditions  Examining                         allowable
                                      trends in        Examining        over limit
                                      interest-bearing liquidity
                                      debts            in hand          Evaluating
                                                                        measures
                                      Examining       Examining         to preserve
                                      free CF         return on         receivables
                                                      equity(ROE)
```

(a) Review the Books

The company must review the Accounts Receivable Ledger on a monthly basis and prepare an Aging Summary to determine the quality of receivables. Generally, there may be a high possibility that the company cannot collect from long past due accounts.

(b) Periodic Review of the Receivable Balance

For recurring transactions, the credit balance can exceed the approved credit limit, if it is not properly monitored. A customer temporary falling behind in payment, a large increase in transaction amount or multiple parallel transactions with the same customer can cause this situation. Thus, management must establish a framework to monitor the receivable balance of the company as a whole in a timely manner. It is also important to compare the receivable balance and credit limit periodically. When an organization gets bigger and more complicated, different departments or different companies within the group may have a different customer code for the same customer.

A unified standard customer code, such as a shared database, shared by all departments and companies within the group can eliminate confusion.

(c) Review External Information

The company must conduct periodic credit investigation and be attentive to external information, such as industry information and word of mouth.

KEYWORD

Credit Investigation: Prior to entering into a sales contract, an investigation on the customer's financial condition and their debt payment situation are conducted to understand and validate the collection risk. Generally, a company may request a credit agency to investigate. However, the company must also analyze and judge self-obtained information, like financial statements, along with second party findings.

Credit Limit: It is the credit ceiling or the maximum amount of sales that a customer is permitted to transact.

Terms and Conditions: They are the contract conditions stated in the Sales Agreement such as the contract amount, delivery date, inspection method, payment method, due date, etc.

Accounts Receivable Ledgers: For the purpose of control, the company should make an account book (subsidiary ledger) for each customer, when working with multiple customers. The company records credit sales and collection of accounts receivable for each customer in the account book.

(2) Contract (Order Taking)/Customer Purchase Orders (PO's)

The company confirms the conditions of the existing credit limits. It should reexamine the contents of the transactions if the credit sales are over the limit.

Terms and conditions of the contract include the contract prices, delivery dates, inspection methods, payment methods, payment due dates, warranty liabilities, etc. One of the important terms is the contract price. The company must inspect the Purchase Order sent by the customer in detail to determine if the terms are in line with the original agreed contract and there's no unfavorable conditions, if not they need to be revised.

Regulatory compliance is involved in any kind of transaction. The contract content needs to be reviewed in detail to ensure regulatory compliance. If there are any terms or conditions that may be disadvantageous to the company, the company must request the customer to modify them accordingly. If necessary the company should request legal support on contract review.

(3) Posting of Sales

The company should refer to the accounting standard it uses when sale of goods is posted.

According to IFRS, the revenue from the sales of goods is recognized if all five of the following criteria are met:

(a) The significant risks and rewards of ownership of the goods are transferred to the buyer,
(b) The entity (or seller) does not retain either a continuing managerial involvement or control over the goods,
(c) The amount of revenue can be measured reliably,
(d) Probable economic benefits will flow to the entity from the transaction, and
(e) The costs incurred can be measured reliably.

According to USGAAP, the revenue, whether from the sale of product or provision of services, is generally recognized if all four of the following criteria are met:

(a) Persuasive evidence of an arrangement exists,
(b) Delivery has occurred or services have been rendered,
(c) The seller's price to the buyer is fixed or determinable, and
(d) Collectability is reasonably assured.

1. Accounts Receivable Management

It should be noted that the Revenue Standard is currently being updated under IFRS and US GAAP, so this definition could change in the future periods.

(4) Billing/Invoicing

After confirming that the goods were transferred to a customer, the company will demand payment based on the agreed terms of the appropriately authorized contract. In some countries, a Proof of Delivery (POD) or Delivery Receipt with signature of customer is required to demand payment. In such cases, company needs to set up a rule to collect PODs and attach them to the invoices for collection.

The company should prepare the billing/invoicing based on the Shipping Order or Sales Slip and deliver it to the customer. Depending on customer's terms and conditions, two different timings for billing/invoicing delivery can be used:
1. Individual Billing/Invoicing – Billing/Invoicing attached individually with the delivery of goods and the Delivery Receipt
2. Aggregate Billing/Invoicing – an aggregate billing/invoicing of the transaction for the whole month in the form of a Monthly Statement of Account

(5) Settlement/Payment

The company must confirm the receipt of money, validate it with the corresponding bill, and then process the settlement.

Once the payment is received, the corresponding receivable/debtor should be reversed (apply cash receipt). When issuing bills/invoices with the same amount on a monthly basis or billing/invoicing multiple customers with the same amount, the company must carefully review them to avoid reconciliation errors by matching invoice number to dispatch note number.

2. Receivable Management by Customer
(1) Receivables Management by Customer

In order to properly understand the receivable balance, the company should prepare an Accounts Receivable Ledger for each customer (Subsidiary Receivable Ledger). This will also be used as a source for the credit management.

Management must identify customers that have outstanding receivables. They must send the Accounts Receivable Balance Confirmation Letter to the customer to check/confirm the actual receivable balance status. Afterwards, they should collect the response, collate the information and prepare a summary. In addition, since the crucial part of receivables management is in collection, they must prepare a Monitoring Sheet for Collection to check the collection status usually referred to as the aged debtor report.

[Management of collecting AR(Accounts Receivable)]

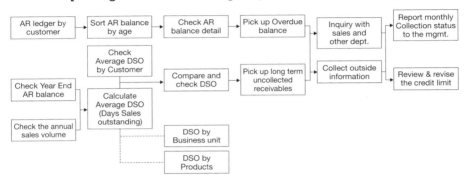

(2) Receivables Management by Due Date

To understand the credit risk involved for each customer, the company must investigate unpaid receivables by sorting the outstanding receivables by settlement/due date. This is referred to as the "Aging" or "Aging Test".

The company must confirm the reason why the receivable was not paid at the settlement date. Long-term uncollected receivables are separately managed and monitored. An Aging List categorizes outstanding receivable balances by the number of months it has not been paid. At an early stage, management can identify any slow-downs and abnormal delays in collection from customers.

(3) Treatment of Delinquent Receivables

If there are Delinquent Receivables, the company needs to decide what action should be taken based on the current situation of the customer.

- Establish contacts in customer payment department
- Email aged debt to customer for confirmation
- Follow up by phone call
- Request internal sales/logistics support if issue is internal
- Repeat email/phone call
- Formal demand

- Threat of non-supply

If there is still no payment received, management should conduct a review of the transaction volume, settlement situation and materiality of the balances. They should consider terminating the engagement as soon as possible and send it to the legal department for litigation. However, litigation is a last resort and should be reviewed in light of the size, scale and importance of the customer on a global basis to the supplier and its global organization. Also, litigation may outweigh the debt balance and therefore may not be worth pursuing.

3. Sales Discount and Rebates
(1) Treatment of Sales Discount and Rebates

Management should refer to the agreed contract and ensure compliance with company policy on sales allowances and rebates.

> **KEYWORD**
> - **Sales Allowance**: A credit given to price of a sold product due to lack of weight, defective or damaged product.
> - **Rebates**: The partial return of a payment of a sale when a purchase is above the specified quantity, or value.
> - **Sales Discount**: The sales price reduction usually offered when a customer pays prior to the due date.

(2) Payment/Debit note

There is a way to directly pay the sales allowance and rebate to the customer. The company should prepare a Payment Request based on the approved sales discount or rebate and process the payment.

Accounting Key Points

1. Recognition

Accounts receivable is recognized when sales transaction occurs. There are several types of sales transactions. The company should follow the accounting standards the company adopts, when it considers how to recognize the sales revenue and accounts receivable.

The timing of recognizing sales can be as follows.
(a) When shipped the product
(b) When delivered the product
(c) When inspection by customer has completed
(d) At the time of payment collection

If the sale is made under FOB shipping point terms, the seller is supposed to record both the sales transaction and related charges to the cost of goods sold at the time when the shipment leaves its port/shipping dock. From that point onward, the delivery is technically the responsibility of either a third-party shipper or the buyer.

If the sale is made under FOB destination terms, the seller is supposed to record the sales transaction and related charges to the cost of goods sold at the time when the shipment arrives at the customer. The delivery is still the responsibility of the seller until it reaches the customer's location.

From a practical perspective, many companies record their sales transactions as though the delivery terms are FOB shipping point. It becomes easier to verify. Recording the transaction upon arrival at the customer requires substantially more work to verify.

There are other sales transactions such as Outsourcing/Consignment sales, Installment sales, etc.
In long-term construction contracts which span more than one accounting period, the Percentage of Completion Method is a basis for revenue recognition. In case of long-term contracts, accountants need a basis to apportion the total contract revenue between the multiple accounting periods. The Percentage of Completion Method provides one basis and the full/completed-contract method provides another.

2. Evaluation

If the company sells on credit, customers will occasionally be unable to pay. Accounting should charge those accounts receivables to expense as a bad debt.

ts arise and accrue an expense
1. Accounts Receivable Management

They should estimate the amount of bad debt that might arise and accrue an expense for it at the end of each reporting period. The debit is listed in the bad debt expense account, which causes an expense to appear in the income statement. The credit is listed in the allowance for bad debts account, which is a reserve account that appears in the balance sheet. Later, when a specific invoice is clearly identifiable as a bad debt, the accounts receivable is removed with a credit, and the reserve is reduced with a debit.

If the customer were to pay the invoice later, accounting would simply reverse the entry, so that the allowance account is increased back to its former level.

An alternative method is the direct write-off method, where a bad debt expense is recognized when a specific invoice that will not to be paid is identified. Under this approach, debit the bad debt expense and credit the accounts receivable/debtors account avoiding the use of an allowance account. This is not the preferred method for recording bad debts, because it introduces a delay between the recognition of a sale and the recognition of any related bad debt expense (which violates the matching principle).

3. Journal Entries
(1) Sales on Credit
Depending on how the tax is recorded, the following are the journal entries when there is a sale on credit for an item amounting to 1,000 Yen plus 10% value added tax;

Dr) Accounts Receivable 1,100	Cr) Sales 1,000
	Output tax 100

(2) Collection
Collection may be done through cash, cheque or bank deposits/transfers. The appropriate entry for the collection is as follows:

Dr) Cash xxx	Cr) Accounts Receivable xxx

The company can encourage customers to pay early by offering a discount. If the customer takes advantage of the discount, the payment will be less than the invoice total. The discount is shown as a reduction of profit as follows:

| Dr) Cash | xxx | Cr) Accounts Receivable | xxx |
| Sales Discount | xxx | | |

(3) Uncollectible Receivables

Unfortunately, some sales on account may not be collected, in spite of the best efforts of the sales, accounting, and legal departments and counsels. Failure of collection is recorded as uncollectible items, or "Bad Debts".

DIRECT WRITE-OFF METHOD

The direct write-off method is a simple method to account for uncollectible accounts. A specific account receivable is removed from the accounting records at the time it is finally determined to be uncollectible. This method is acceptable when bad debts are not material. It can also be for tax purposes, where tax rules often stipulate that a direct write-off approach is to be used.

The appropriate entry for the direct write off approach is as follows:

| Dr) Bad Debt Expense | xxx | Cr) Accounts Receivable | xxx |

ALLOWANCE METHOD

Allowance method must be used, except when bad debts are not material and for tax purposes where tax rules often stipulate that a direct write-off approach is to be used.

(i) Accounting period end

| Dr) Bad Debt Expense | 1,000 | Cr) Bad Debts Allowance | 1,000 |

(ii) When collection of Accounts receivable failed for 800
  → In case Bad Debts Allowance balance is 1,000

| Dr) Bad Debts Allowance | 800 | Cr) Accounts Receivable | 800 |

  → In case Bad Debts Allowance balance is 600

| Dr) Bad Debts Allowance | 600 | Cr) Accounts Receivable | 800 |
| Bad Debt Expense | 200 | | |

Internal Control Key Points

1. Credit Management

The department that sets the credit limit, like the Finance or the Collection Department, should be independent of the Sales Department. This prevents the risk of arbitrary credit limits for new customers and unauthorized adjustment or altering of the approved credit limit for new and existing customer. This also ensures the implementation of the established policy.

2. Contact (Order Taking)

The Credit Administrator should develop a monitoring worksheet that can determine the balance of credit still available for customers. This ensures that credit sales approval is within the set limit. Customer master states the credit limit and the Subsidiary Receivable Ledger states the outstanding/unpaid account balances. The monitoring sheet data should be based on the Customer Master and the Subsidiary Receivable Ledger. If applicable, it is ideal to set the credit limit for each customer in the IT system so that no entry exceeds the limit.

3. Posting of Sales

The person in charge ensures that the amount on all of the attached supporting documents evidencing the sales transactions are consistent, such as Shipping Order and the Sales Slip. This prevents incorrect reporting of sale amounts due to wrong quantities and unit prices.

4. Billing/Invoicing

(i) To prevent tampering and for error detection on Billing/Invoicing, an employee (usually from finance department) independent of sales, collection and logistics sends the Billing/Invoices. That employee is also responsible for validating the accuracy of the amount posted in the Subsidiary Receivable Ledger. This prevents tampering and allows error detection for Billings/Invoices.

(ii) The authorized personnel should review and approve the Billing/Invoices at the time of issuance.

(iii) Check the completeness of issued Billing/Invoices by matching the Subsidiary Receivable Ledger with the Sales Register.

5. Settlement

The person in charge should verify the Deposit Details with the Receivables Balance Detail and the books to ensure that there is no omitted or unrecorded item. This prevents incomplete postings of vouchers when offsetting, such as the Credit Memo.

6. Receivable Management by Customer

The person in charge should check if the supporting documents match with the amount posted in the Subsidiary Receivable Ledger. This prevents incomplete recording of sales data in the subsidiary ledger. This will ensure that there is no omission or unrecorded transaction.

7. Treatment of Delinquent Receivables/Doubtful Accounts

An investigation can determine the causes for any receivables that remain unpaid within the time allowed by the company. Ideally, the department independent from sales, like Accounting or Finance, should investigate. This assigned department should monitor and supervise collection conducted by the Sales Department.

8. Treatment of Sales Allowance and Rebates

Sales Discounts and Rebates do not involve product movement. This area is susceptible to fraud and deserves extra caution.

Accordingly, the following internal control points should be considered:

(i) The person in charge of sales should complete the appropriate application. Afterwards, he or she should obtain the approval from the appropriate authorized officer and conduct the settlement. Supporting documents for the calculation should be cross-checked, such as vouchers and contracts.
(ii) Settlement should be conducted through bank transfer or by offsetting. However, cash payment should be avoided as much as possible.

Tips for Good Accounting Practices!

- There is a strong desire for the Sales Department to increase their sales. Internal controls will prevent posting of fictitious sale such as matching invoices and dispatch notes.
- Be vigilant until the receivables are collected. A monitoring mechanism such as an aged debt report enables management to have a timely understanding of the status of uncollected receivables. This also mitigates the risk of bad debt.
- For the allowance for doubtful accounts, corporate accounting and tax have different input requirements. In many cases for accounting, allowances are set aside in advance. However, for taxes, the tax effect of the amount that was not recognized is to be recognized as deferred tax assets.

2. Accounts Payable Management

Accounts payable refers to obligations of a business to its vendors for services and purchases, such as goods and raw materials, and through settlement by payment of the amount.

This chapter will explore topics on management of payables for the purchase of physical goods and services, including trade and non-trade payables. Expense Payables shall be discussed at Expense Management chapter.

Process Flow

Supplier Management 〉 Purchase Contract 〉 Purchase 〉 Payable Management by Due Date 〉 Settlement

1. Supplier Management
(1) Selection of Supplier

The purpose of the purchasing operations is to establish a system for ensuring a stable and continuous supply of goods from reliable suppliers by purchasing products at reasonable prices, in an appropriate quantity, and within any specified delivery period, to specific standards.

Therefore, it is important to select and register approved suppliers. For the selection of these suppliers, it is also important to keep updated information, including any information gained through financial statements, periodic credit investigations and customer reviews, and any industry information.

A. New Suppliers

Before the company starts a business with a new supplier, the company should set up a Policy on Supplier selection. The Policy on Supplier selection can be used to determine if the supplier can be trusted for its reliability to deliver goods and services. The company should also establish standard terms and conditions of purchase, which will include a Policy on Payment that will inform the supplier about the company's requirements before the release of payment to them. The purchasing

2. Accounts Payable Management

department should make sure the supplier selection process is followed and that suppliers sign to the company's standard terms and conditions. (These terms and conditions should be checked by your legal advisors for completeness and effectiveness)

(a) Supplier Selection
Getting quotes from multiple suppliers, reviewing the price including terms and conditions, and selecting the appropriate one. The criteria for selection of supplier should be based, not only on price, but also on other factors such as: 1) after service warranty and 2) availability of spare parts.

(b) Setting up of an Approved Suppliers List
Collect the following information from the suppliers: 1) evidence of the existence of the company (e. g. Registration and Statutory Reports); 2) financial information (e. g. Financial Statement and Income Tax Returns); 3) trade referrals; and 4) other information needed for suppliers' accreditation. 5) Credit agency reports.

Set up the Approved Suppliers List based on Suppliers' Accreditation, approved by the management or the appropriate authority. This should be based on the approved contract. File the collected documents as support to the Approved Suppliers List. It is ideal that a service level contract/terms and conditions be signed by the supplier. Accordingly, it is good practice that the payment should be released based on the authorized criteria in compliance with the payment policy within the companies standard terms and conditions.

B. Existing Suppliers
For existing supplier, a periodic review of supplier's financial statements should be done to determine its liquidity (short-term capacity to pay) and solvency (long-term capacity to pay).
A periodic review of the service level agreement should also be conducted. It should consider the quality, delivery time, cost and after sales service support.

2. Purchase Contract
Before engaging with the service or purchase of goods from the supplier, the company needs to secure a signed contract. The contract should cover the basic terms and conditions. In particular, this should include: 1) purpose of trading; 2) contract period; 3) delivery time and terms; 4) payment terms; 5) inspection method;

6) quality assurance; 7) other terms intended by management; 8) warranty; 9) insurance; and 10) non-disclosure agreement.

When making a contract, the company should consider compliance with the existing laws and regulations, applicable to respective country, to ensure contract validity and enforceability.

3. Purchase

There are several standards for purchase recognition:

(1) Acceptance Standard/Goods Receipt

Acceptance standard/goods receipt is a method of recording the purchase of goods at the time it is actually received. At the time of receipt of goods, it is important to prepare standard forms to communicate with the purchasing-related departments and maintain their internal control. Documents to be created or obtained are delivery receipts and invoices. The company needs to confirm the dates on which the documents were created or obtained. These documents should be classified by date or per supplier. The purchasing-related departments must also check these documents against a copy of Purchase Order and other related documents.

In the purchase ledger book, the company needs to confirm that the payment amount is correct by cross-checking the delivery receipts, the purchase order and the invoices.

(2) Inspection Standard

Inspection standard is the method of recording the purchase at the time of inspecting and accepting the goods. Inspection Standard is a way to record the purchase, after it is confirmed that there are no defective or wrong specification goods at the time of receipt. This method is the most reliable and common method for accounts payable management.

As described in (1) Acceptance Standard, preparing a standard form and keeping organized filing are required. The following documents should be created or obtained:

(i) Inspection Report — Inspection process should be conducted by using acceptance reports with sequential numbers. A copy of it should be circulated to the relevant departments.

(ii) Receiving Report — Insufficient quantity and poor quality should be specified in this report and a copy of the report should be circulated to the relevant departments.
(iii) Delivery Receipt and Invoice — These documents should be checked against a copy of the Purchase Order and a copy of the Inspection Report by the relevant departments.
(iv) Return Slip and Receipt of Returned Goods — The authorized representative of the supplier should sign to Receipt of Returned Goods as proof that the goods are being returned. Both documents are required to be circulated to the relevant departments, in order to check the quantity, unit price, and other details.

4. Monitoring and Settlement/Payment
(1) Payable Management by Due Date

Payable is recorded at the time of recognition of purchase and the method of payment depends on the company's agreement with the individual supplier (Signed Terms and Conditions). Thus, it is necessary to manage the outstanding payables by due date.

To do this, the company needs to create a payment schedule, which reflects payables by due date, to determine when and to whom the payment should be made. The Payment Schedule enables the company to prevent late payment and double payment and nonpayment. It is important to adopt this schedule for efficient cash management. Aging of payables should be incorporated with the Payment Schedule to monitor if there is any payment that has not been made on the predetermined settlement conditions and that there are no outstanding payables remaining unsettled over a long period of time.

(2) Settlement

Settlement is performed in the following procedure:
(i) Confirmation of the Details of the Invoice and Recognition of Payables: The Invoice should be validated and matched with Purchase Order and Delivery Receipt. The Purchase Order should always be checked, for the cases in which the Sales Invoice does not reflect the discount. Ideally, the following details should be considered: 1) item's description; 2) quantity; 3) unit price; and 4) discount computation. After confirmation, the company records the payable on the basis of the details of the Invoice.

(ii) Request for Payment: The company confirms each supplier's payment terms and prepares the request for payment. This will be the basis for the cheque preparation or direct bank transfer.
(iii) Payment Execution: The company executes the payment to each supplier, according to the Request for Payment.
(iv) Payable Clearing: After payment execution, the company should record its payment on Supplier's Subsidiary. Confirmation should be made by sending the supplier with Payment Advice to inform them that payment has been made.

(3) Payable Management by Supplier

Supplier's Subsidiary allows the company to manage individual payables and helps identify troubles, such as payment delay, double payment, and cancellation. Since this record shows the total payable by the supplier, it is necessary that all payments made to each supplier are reflected in this record.

5. Purchase Returns and Allowances/Purchase Discount
(1) Treatment of Purchase Return and Allowances/Purchase Discount

Refer to the contract and company policy on purchase returns and allowance/purchase discounts and ensure compliance with it.

> **KEYWORD**
>
> - **Purchase Returns and Allowances**: Refers to the amount which is deducted from the invoice amount due to insufficient quantity, poor quality and/or damage on purchasing goods.
> - **Purchase Rebate**: Refers to the refunded amount of the invoice amount received from the supplier when the company has a large amount or a large volume of the purchase transaction for a period of time. It is generally referred to as a rebate.
> - **Purchase Discount**: Refers to reduction of payment amount when the company made a payment within a prescribed time for the purchase transaction. It is generally referred to as a discount.

(2) Settlement

The company confirms that the Payment Request is executed and that the payment has been made.

(3) Official Receipt

The company confirms the details for approval and issues an Official Receipt to the supplier.

Accounting Key Points

1. Recognition

Like the Account Receivables Cycle, there is an issue with the timing of the purchase transaction. This is more serious when importing goods.

If the purchase is made under the term FOB shipping point, the risk and reward are transferred to the buyer at the time of shipment. The buyer records both purchase transaction and related charges as the cost of goods from the time when the shipment leaves the supplier's warehouse or port/shipping dock. From that point, the delivery cost is technically the responsibility of the buyer.

If the sale is made under the term FOB destination, the risk and reward are transferred to the buyer upon receipt of the goods. The seller is supposed to record these transactions when the shipment arrives at the buyer. This is because the delivery is still the responsibility of the seller, until it reaches its intended destination. From the buyer's point of view, the purchase transaction shall be recognized when the shipment arrives.

From a practical perspective, many companies record their purchase transactions as though the delivery terms were FOB destination, due to ease of verification. Recording the transaction when the shipment leaves its shipping dock requires substantially more work to verify and it is usually done at the end of each period for adjustment of purchase transactions, if any. However if the company does take ownership of the goods at this point verification is important for insurance purposes.

When recording a purchase at the destination, there are still three different timing as follows;

Recognition Policy	Point of Recognition
Receipt Basis	When the goods arrived
Inspection Basis	When the goods are inspected and accepted
Consumption Basis	When the buyer consumed the goods. Only the portion of goods accepted in the warehouse and actually consumed in the operation are recognized as purchased.

Any recognition policy can be adopted internally by a company, as far as the policy to be applied consistently however safest is on receipt

2. Cost of Purchase

The cost of purchase of inventory is comprised of the purchase price, import duties and other taxes (other than those subsequently recoverable by the entity from the taxing authorities), freight cost, handling cost and other costs directly attributable to the acquisition of finished goods, materials and services. Trade discounts, rebates and other similar items are deducted in determining the costs of purchase.

You may purchase inventories on deferred settlement terms. In some cases, the arrangement effectively contains an unstated financing element, for example, a difference between the purchase price for normal credit terms and the deferred settlement amount. In these cases, the difference is recognized as interest expense over the period of the financing.

3. Special Types of Purchases
(1) Drop Ship

You can ask your supplier to ship goods directly to your customer, instead of delivering the goods to you. This type of shipment is called a drop ship or drop shipment. You will record your purchase based on the delivery receipt. (The carrier and or customer should supply you with proof of delivery "POD")

(2) Purchase at Suppliers Warehouse

A company may arrange with suppliers to purchase goods at the supplier's warehouse. The purchase may be recorded based on statement of delivery from the supplier. As there is no movement of goods, there may be no inspection. The risks involved in the ownership of goods may be vague.

You should check the inventory control over the goods, the necessity of the transaction, the terms and conditions, as well as any supporting documents, such as the purchase order and the warehouse bill, to avoid any fraud or mismanagement involved in this type of purchase.

(3) Purchase without Determining the Price

In practice, there are cases where the cost of goods shall be determined after the delivery of goods. An example is that the ownership of goods is transferred to a buyer at a shipping point, but the cost is to be determined at the percentage of the market price at the destination. It is ideal to record the purchase at an estimated cost of goods and adjust the difference later on to avoid any accounting fraud to control the timing of recognition.

4. Journal Entries
(1) Purchase on Credit

When there was a purchase of goods for sale on credit amounting 100 plus 10% value added tax, journal entries are as follows depends on how the tax shall be recorded;

1. Inclusive of sales tax

| Dr) Purchases | 110 | Cr) Accounts Payable — Trade | 110 |

2. Exclusive of sales tax

| Dr) Purchases | 100 | Cr) Accounts Payable — Trade | 110 |
| Dr) Input Tax | 10 | | |

(2) Payment

Payment may be done through cash, check or bank deposits. The appropriate entry for the collection is as follows:

| Dr) Accounts Payable — Trade | xxx | Cr) Cash | xxx |

If the supplier offers a discount, the buyer should take advantage of it since the required payment will be less than the total invoice price.

The discount is shown as a reduction of Accounts Payable — Trade as follows:

Dr) Accounts Payable — Trade	xxx	Cr) Cash	xxx
		Cr) Purchase Discount	xxx

Internal Control Key Points

1. Inspection

For purposes of internal control, inspection must be done by another person who is not involved in the preparation of Purchase Order.

In addition, it is necessary to cross-check receipt certificates such as Statement of Delivery with the Contract or Purchase Order, and to confirm that the details of the receipt of goods are consistent with those of the Purchase Order.

2. Settlement - (Segregation of Duties)

Payment processing must be done by a person other than the person in charge of the purchasing. It is important to maintain the internal check process by separating the duties of the person performing the payment and those of the person responsible for approval of the payment. In addition, to prevent errors in the addresses of payees and the amount of payment, cross-checking of the payment request form and the invoice is necessary. After payment, the payment personnel should conduct extra precaution to prevent double payment by stamping "paid" on the vouchers and supporting documents.

3. Management of Payable Balance - (By Statement Reconciliations)

The company should periodically inquire about the company's payable to its suppliers. By confirming the outstanding payable to the supplier by the accounting department, the internal checks and balances to the purchasing department will be in place. Since the abnormal balances are often caused by miscommunication between the purchasing department, the inspection department, the accounting department and other departments, it is necessary for the company to efficiently manage each department.

4. Investigation on Outstanding Accounts Payable

It is important to conduct an investigation on outstanding accounts payable, just like for aging receivables, to figure out the cause. Generally, common errors, including bookkeeping error, are considered the cause, but, in the worst case scenario, it may also be due to a fictitious purchase.

 Tips for Good Accounting Practices!

It is important to confirm outstanding payables because it may affect cash management. The company should confirm outstanding payables periodically.
Conduct detailed investigation of outstanding payables. DO NOT record it as miscellaneous expense or sundry expense without finding the cause.

3. Inventory Management

Inventory asset refers to finished goods, manufactured goods, work-in-process products, bought out components and raw materials, which the business holds for the purpose of selling to customers. Proper inventory management is one of the major challenges for the business. Insufficient inventory may result in missing sales opportunities and losing customers, short shipping to customers, inability to manufacture and deliver. On the other hand, holding too much inventory may result in slow-moving inventory, obsolescence and may add more financial burden in the form of storage cost affecting the cash flow. Very often, a huge part of the company's capital may be tied up in the inventory, thus, making the company less liquid. In recent years, inventory management is not only a challenge that business faces, but also a challenge for the Supply Chain Management (SCM) from procurement to production to sales. Therefore, possessing an optimal inventory is a continuous issue for any business. This chapter will explore topics on good practices of inventory management.

Process Flow

1. Balance Management
(1) Balance Management

The company must regularly perform physical inventory (commonly referred as inventory/stock count) and check the consistency between the quantity of the actual stored inventory and the recorded balances. If there is any difference, the company must investigate the cause of the difference and make any necessary adjustments in the accounting records.

> **KEYWORD**
> - **Physical Inventory**: It is the procedure to actually check and count (quantity, weight, etc.) the inventory assets at the end of each fiscal year. This is an important procedure for determining the cost of sales, and at the same time, it helps discover defective, slow moving and obsolete goods as well as recognize the inventory write-downs.

3. Inventory Management

(2) Objective of Physical Inventory Count

Physical inventory is the process required to achieve the following objectives:
(i) From the perspective of financial accounting, which aims for proper periodic accounting of profit and loss, this is an essential means to understand the exact cost of sales.
(ii) By conducting physical inventory, it allows a company to understand the physically, functionally and economically obsolete inventories such as: reject items, damaged items and other items with problems. It also helps to discover inefficient aspects of purchasing, ordering and other functions of the company, which may lead in improving its business practices.

(3) Possible Source of Discrepancy

The possible source of discrepancy between the actual inventory and the inventory assets booked in the accounting records are due to the following reasons:

Actual Inventory	⇐ Occurrence of Difference ⇒	Inventory in Accounting Records

1) Error in actual physical inventory count (ex. Error rate increase when storage/warehouse continues to release or receive goods during the physical counting, especially for fast-moving and big volume goods)
2) Error in tabulation of inventory tag (Bin Card/ Inventory Index Card)
3) Error in actual posting or units used as measure (ex. Counted in meters but recorded as liter)
4) Error in calculation of receipt/issue of inventory/stock transfer slip (Transfer packing Slip)
5) Damage, loss, pilferage, shrinkage, and theft of stock in storage
6) Diversion to other goods, etc.

Causes

1) Error in encoding of Goods Issuance Slip or Goods Receipt Slip (ex. Double entry, incomplete entry, entry error, etc.)
2) Loss of Goods Issuance Slip or Goods Receipt Slip
3) Incomplete processing of sale or transfer
4) Incomplete reporting of sample and disposal
5) Miscalculation or wrong tabulation in book

> **KEYWORD**
>
> - **Inventory Tag (Bin Card/Inventory Index Card)**: At the time of the inventory count, a Warehouse Staff attaches an Inventory Tag to each inventory/stock in preparation for inventory. On the Inventory Tag, there will be a space to fill in information such as the part number, part description, unit, and quantity, inventory/stock checker name and auditor name. To complete the form, the Warehouse Staff should (1) use a ballpoint pen and, (2) if there is an error in entry, not correct the error and mark X on the tag. The Warehouse Staff will then record the error on the Inventory Tag Control Sheet. This procedure prevents a Staff from performing any improper or illegal processing of quantity. Inventory Tags must be in sequential order.

【Process Flow of Verification of Physical Inventory】

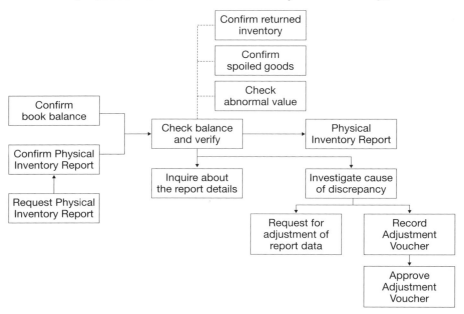

3. Inventory Management

2. Management of Inventory/Stock Receipt and Inventory/Stock Issuance

Inventory/Stock receiving process is a procedure to inspect and record incoming goods, while inventory/stock issuance/dispatch process is a procedure to inspect and record outgoing goods.

(1) Management of Inventory/Stock Receipt and Inventory/Stock Issuance

By understanding what the incoming goods (purchase) or outgoing goods (sale) are, the quantity and value of inventory assets can be properly managed. Once the quantity is determined, a company values the inventory based on the unit cost specified by the valuation method adopted by the company.

Managing the Inventory/Stock Receiving and the Inventory/Stock Issuance process is the first step for conducting an accurate inventory management. The following are the benefits of proper management:

(i) Understanding the accuracy of the inventory balance.
(ii) Maintaining an appropriate level of inventory.
(iii) Performing smooth purchasing and delivering activities.

A. Calculation of Amount

Amount of inventory is commonly determined by Perpetual Inventory System or Periodic Inventory System.

Perpetual Inventory System	In this method, the receipt/issue and balance for each item is recorded. Thus, the inventory account balance is always recorded. By regularly performing inventory count and verifying the book with the actual inventory, the inventory discrepancies are identified. The Inventory/Stock Ledger is a sub-ledger that a company uses that allows a company to manage inventory assets. Formulas: Previous term carried over quantity + current term purchase quantity - net issued quantity = current term physical inventory quantity
Periodic Inventory System	In this method, the inventory is not recorded during the term. Instead, the inventory count is conducted at the end of the period. Compared to the perpetual inventory system, this method entails less work. However, if there is inventory shrinkage, the quantity of the shrinkage will be included in the issued quantity. As a result, this may not be a sufficient method of inventory management. Formulas: Previous term carried over quantity + current term purchase quantity - inventory count quantity = current term issued quantity

B. Calculation of Unit Price
Refer to page 32 **Accounting Key Points 3. Measurement of Inventories**.

(2) Verification of Inventory/Stock Issuance and Inventory/Stock Receiving

The company needs to verify that the Inventory/Stock Issuance and Inventory/Stock Receiving process comply with internal standards and company policies. It should investigate any discrepancies with the relevant departments, report the discrepancies results, and conduct appropriate adjustments accordingly.

【Process Flow of Inventory/Stock Issuance and Inventory/Stock Receiving】

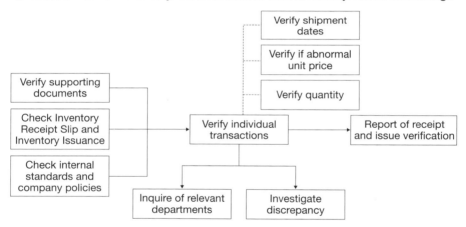

3. Maintaining Proper Inventory Level

Proper inventory level refers to minimizing the cost, such as storage cost while neither causing a shortage of inventory nor an excess of inventory. In order to maintain proper inventory level, it is necessary to perform inventory management by controlling quantity and age (inventory period).

(1) Setting of Proper Inventory Level

A. Setting the Minimum Inventory Level
Safety Inventory/Stock: This is a way to determine the quantity target of inventory based on the level of inventory, which does not hinder the sales and the manufacturing

3. Inventory Management

departments' activities, due to a shortage of products or inventory/stocks (determined by part and by supply chain lead times). Even if there is any additional order or defective products over the expected amount of sales, there would be enough inventory. It is important to set company standards for inventory turnover ratio, taking the delivery period and sales plan into consideration.

B. Inventory Cost
Storage costs, insurance, transportation fees, expenses arising due to obsolescence and supplies expenses should be considered when computing the amount of safety inventory/stock.

(2) Verification of Appropriate Inventory

A. Quantity
Check the pre-set standard inventory/purchase order quantity and actual inventory quantity to determine the difference. Contact the relevant department, investigate the cause of the discrepancy and execute countermeasures.

B. Age
In addition to the aspect of quantity, the management of inventory has an additional aspect, age (inventory period). If the quantity meets the criteria, but there is no movement of the inventory, the quality may be deteriorated (especially perishable items) and become expired inventory/stock.

In actual procedure, after comparing a predetermined reference age of inventory (period) with the actual age of inventory and confirming any excess content, it is necessary to investigate the cause of excess. Afterward, create a countermeasure plan and implement it.

C. Method of Setting the Criteria for Inventory Age
The company needs to take the industries and business categories and the environmental and seasonal variations into account. Then, set the criteria for managing the period that has elapsed from the time of purchase. For example, if the period from purchase order to delivery is short, it is possible to shorten the inventory age. If the period is long and not affected by seasonal variations, it is possible to set a longer period as the criteria.

> **KEYWORD**
>
> - **Inventory Turnover Ratio**: An indicator for checking whether excess or slow moving inventory occurs. It is possible to determine whether the product is superior or inferior, by computing it per product. Higher inventory turnover indicates higher sales and more efficient production. This means that the product sells well.
>
> **Formula:**
> Inventory turnover ratio = Inventory Issued amount ÷ Inventory amount
> In the company whose main business is trading or distribution, it is also necessary to manage the turnover ratio on a company-wide basis.
>
> **Formula: Inventory Turnover Ratio = Sales ÷ average inventory/stock amount at the beginning and end of the term.**
> In addition, it is also possible to obtain the number of days of slow moving inventory by replacing the inventory turnover ratio with the number of days.
>
> **Formula:**
> Inventory turnover period (days) = 365 ÷ inventory turnover ratio

Accounting Key Points

1. Scope of Inventories

IFRS defines inventories as follows:
(a) Assets held for sale in the ordinary course of business;
(b) Assets in the process of production for such sales (work in process); or
(c) Assets in the form of materials or supplies to be consumed in the production process or in the rendering of services.

USGAAP defines inventories as follows:
(a) Assets held for sale in the ordinary course of business;
(b) Assets in process of production for such sales (work in process); or
(c) Assets to be currently consumed in the production of goods or services to be available for sale.

3. Inventory Management

Depending on the type of business of your company, inventories may include the following:
(a) Work in progress arising under construction contracts, including directly related service contracts (see Section 1 Account Receivables) or as part of a production process
(b) Financial instruments; and
(c) Biological assets related to agricultural activity and agricultural produce at the point of harvest.

Please take note that these types of inventory need special treatment from an accounting perspective. Special care may be also required for inventory in accordance to the taxation law of your country.

2. Cost of Inventories

Cost of inventories shall include all costs of purchase, costs of conversion and other costs incurred in bringing the inventories to their present location and condition.

A. Costs of Purchase

The costs of purchase of inventories are comprised of the purchase price, import duties and other taxes (other than those subsequently recoverable by the entity from the taxing authorities), as well as transport, handling and other costs directly attributable to the acquisition of finished goods, materials and services.
When determining the costs of purchase, trade discounts, rebates and other similar items are deducted.

B. Costs of Conversion

The costs of conversion of inventories include costs directly related to the units of production, such as direct labor and equipment. They also include a systematic allocation of fixed and variable production overheads that are incurred in converting materials into finished goods.

C. Other Costs

An entity shall include other costs in the cost of inventories only to the extent that they are incurred in bringing the inventories to their present location and condition.

Examples of costs excluded from the cost of inventories and recognized as expenses in the period in which they are incurred are;

(a) Abnormal amounts of wasted materials (scrap over standard), labor or other production costs;
(b) Storage costs, unless those costs are necessary during the production process before a further production stage;
(c) Administrative overheads that do not contribute to bringing inventories to their present location and condition; and
(d) Selling costs.

3. Measurement of Inventories

Inventories can be measured using the First-In, First-Out (FIFO), method or the weighted average method, etc., based on the accounting standard. These methods are adopted for inventories with similar natures and uses to the entity in IFRS. Unlike IFRS, the same methods need not to be adopted to inventories with similar natures and uses to the entity in US GAAP.
For inventories with different natures or uses, different cost formulas may be justified. However, the Last-In, First-Out method (LIFO) is not permitted by IFRS.
You shall measure the cost of inventories of items that are not ordinarily interchangeable as well as goods or services produced and segregated for specific projects, by using specific identification of their individual costs.

At the end of each reporting period, you shall measure inventories at the lower of cost and Net realizable value (estimated selling price less costs to complete and sell) in IFRS, and lower of cost or Market in US GAAP. You may use techniques for measuring costs such as following;

3. Inventory Management

Cost Measuring Method	Description
Specific Identification Method	Specific costs are attributed to identified items of inventory. This is the appropriate treatment for items that are segregated for a specific project, regardless of whether they have been bought or produced.
Weighted Average Method	Cost of each item is determined from the weighted average of the cost of similar items at the beginning of a period and the cost of similar items purchased or produced during the period.
First-in, First-out Method (FIFO)	FIFO formula assumes that the items of inventory that were purchased or produced first are sold first, and consequently the items remaining in inventory at the end of the period are those most recently purchased or produced.
Last-in, First-out Method (LIFO)	Use most recent purchase price at the time of the accounting period end for measuring the cost of inventories. This is allowed when the result approximates cost. This method is not permitted to be used by IFRS.
Retail Method	Measures cost by reducing the sales value of the inventory by the appropriate percentage of gross margin.
Standard Cost Method	Use standard cost determined and regularly reviewed by normal levels of materials, supplies, labor, efficiency and capacity utilization.

Internal Control Key Points

1. Balance Management
(1) Proper Processing of Physical Inventory

In order to properly proceed with the implementation of a physical inventory count, the company should prepare specific guidelines such as inventory count schedule, location map of goods, Implementation Report and Inventory Count Procedures/Implementation Guidelines. The guidelines should include procedures when differences occur. The people involved should be familiar with these procedures.

When performing physical inventory at the end of the term, it is important to manage the schedule because it is necessary to complete both an investigation on the cause of difference and the correcting process in a short period of time. To ensure that there is no error in the computation, an employee, not involved in the initial computations, needs to verify the result of the inventory count and perform the recalculation procedure of the amount.

(2) Efficient Inventory Management Based on Physical Inventory

In addition to confirming the quantity of inventory during the physical inventory, the company must optimize inventories by identifying bad inventory, excessive inventory or slow-moving inventory. It is also necessary to manage excessive or slow-moving inventory according to the specific company criteria for processing items and delivery periods. Furthermore, if the storage site is in an external location, it is necessary that the company obtains a confirmation letter to determine that deposit inventories are securely stored in the company's sales warehouse and/or the premises of the suppliers. It is also ideal to go physically to the storage site to recognize its current status. This double-checking might determine potential illegal practices.

2. Verification of Inventory/Stock Issues and Inventory/Stock Receiving

It is necessary to create a unified standard and company criteria for inventory/stock verification. The criteria should include classification and evaluation procedures. This may include policies and procedures adopted by management for handling the inventory assets as well as storage of supporting documents (e.g. vouchers and other documents created at the time of delivery and receipt of inventory assets). The verification of transactions, according to the processing criteria, must be conducted periodically.

(1) Physical Security

Restricting the entry and exit of the warehouse where inventory is stored and taking a record of the entry and exit are recommended to prevent theft and for health and safety. For particularly expensive inventories, physical security devices should be installed.

(2) Cross-Checking of Inventory/Stock Receipt and Inventory/Stock Issue Records

It is necessary to verify dates, price and quantity on the inventory/stock receipt and the inventory/stock issue records with supporting vouchers.

3. Proper Inventory Level Management

(1) The System to Recognize the Quantity Exceeding the Safety Inventory/Stock

Regular comparison of the safety inventory/stock and the actual quantity on hand is necessary to verify if there is a large discrepancy in the inventory. It is recommended to conduct this verification process, according to the unified company standard and criteria, by applying the method of verifying either all items or some major items. It is important to establish the system for recognizing any inventory that exceeds the criteria in a timely manner.

(2) Measures to Solve the Problem with Excessive Inventory

If there is any excessive inventory, it is necessary to restrict, reduce or cancel (if possible) future orders until back in line with the company's sales plan. If there is any difference at warehouse unit level, develop a plan to solve the problem with the relevant departments, by diverting some inventory/stocks to another warehouse, as well as provide guidance, promotion and progress management.

(3) Measures to Solve the Problem with the Quantity Exceeding the Inventory Age

When slow moving inventory has exceeded the inventory age, the company will need to investigate the cause with the relevant departments and develop a plan to solve the problem. It is ideal to analyze the cause by figuring out if it is due to wrong sales prediction, excessive purchase, or some other reason. If the problem is caused by a decline in market price or obsolescence of products, the inventory should be written-down, and it is necessary to ensure that the computation method of write-down is in accordance with the company policy and standard. All inventory write-down should be properly documented and recorded. The slow-moving inventory will result in increased storage and administrative costs that will result in a greater increase in total cost. Therefore, a company should be committed to the earliest possible solution of the problem.

Tips for Good Accounting Practices!

- The management of inventory assets enables a company to improve cash flow/improve free cash.
- Reliable management of product, recording and physical inventory is important for proper management of inventory.
- The Last-In-First-Out (LIFO) Method is not permitted to be used in IFRS.

4. Fixed Asset Management

Fixed assets are classified into three categories: (1) "Tangible fixed assets" that have physical forms such as land, building, furniture and fixtures; (2) "Intangible fixed asset" that do not have physical forms, such as patent rights and software; and (3) "Investment and other assets" that are the investment in long-term financial assets such as investment in securities. In this chapter, tangible assets will be discussed.

Tangible fixed assets often require relatively large amounts of expenditure. They are not recorded as outright expense. Instead, they are capitalized in the year they are purchased. These assets are expensed when they are depreciated in a systematic allocation and, depending on the company's policy, over its estimated useful life. Since fixed assets are used over a longer period of time, regular repairs and maintenance are needed to maintain these assets.
On the other hand, intangible assets are transferable rights with legal basis and economic value. Although they do not have a physical form, they can be directly used for the operation. Intangible assets include leasehold, patent, trademark, utility model rights, goodwill, software, and other legal rights.

【Types of Fixed Asset】

Type	Detail	Account
Tangible fixed asset	Asset with a physical form that a company holds for the purpose of long-term use for more than one year.	Buildings and attached facilities, structures, machinery and equipment, ship, aircraft, vehicle and transport equipment, tools, furniture and fixtures, land, construction in progress, etc.
Intangible fixed asset	A non-physical asset with transferable rights which have legal property rights or economic value, and can be directly used for operation.	Patent, utility model rights, design rights, trademark, goodwill (trade rights), facility use rights, mining rights, fishing rights, dam use rights, water rights, software, leasehold, etc.
Investments and other assets	Other fixed assets that are neither tangible fixed assets nor intangible fixed assets.	Investment securities, stock of an affiliated company, long-term loans, etc.

Process flow

All fixed assets have a useful life. Their life cycle starts from the "Acquisition Phase", continues with the "Management & Maintenance Phase" and always ends with the "Disposal Phase".

Acquisition of Fixed Asset → Management and Maintenance of Fixed Asset → Disposal of Fixed Asset

1. Acquisition of Fixed Asset
(1) Application of Asset Acquisition
Normally, the procedures of fixed asset acquisition are conducted in accordance with the internal standard and company policy. Based on details of the request, the following are verified:

A. Consider the method of raising funds for the purchase and the amount to be raised
When acquiring an asset, the funds raised to acquire them are tied to the asset for a long period of time. Thus, when funds are sourced through loans, the period of long-term loans are according to the estimated useful life of the asset. In a large scale investment, such as the construction of a new factory, the funds may be raised by issuing corporate bonds, by increasing the capital, by borrowing, etc.

B. Accounting treatment during and after the time of acquisition of assets
To determine asset acquisition, the company must ensure that this acquisition is expected to create a cash flow exceeding the amount of investment. The capital appraisal should include assessment by tools such as payback, ROI, NPV, IRR, etc. The interest burden caused by borrowing and the recognition of depreciation cost may impact the income statement in the future. This must be taken into account. The accounting process conducted during and after the acquisition of assets is determined, which verifies its profitability.

4. Fixed Asset Management

(2) Execution of Asset Acquisition
After the acquisition of fixed assets is approved, the assets are acquired following the company policy, usually in the following procedures:

(i) **Purchase order**: Obtain quotation from different vendors; review the price, terms and conditions; and select the appropriate supplier. Depending on scale of project e.g. building a factory then a full scale tender process may be required (requiring architects and surveyors).

(ii) **Inspection**: Upon receipt of fixed assets, check the Purchase Order and Delivery Receipt then perform physical inspection. The asset should then be commissioned as ready for operation.

(iii) **Posting of Asset**: Check the total acquisition costs comprised of the following: the amount of money required for purchase of the fixed asset, the cost incidental to the acquisition and other miscellaneous costs. Record it in the appropriate asset account with a designated fixed asset number within the Fixed Asset Ledger for its physical control.

(iv) **Payment**: Execute payment request based on the invoice of the acquisition of fixed asset.

An accounts payable personnel and a bookkeeping personnel are responsible for payment and recording, respectively.

2. Management and Maintenance of Fixed Asset
(1) Management of Fixed Asset
After the acquisition of fixed asset, the company needs to record it in the Fixed Asset Ledger. The Fixed Asset Ledger is a book provided for the purpose of management of fixed asset. To identify the registered assets, this book records the asset number, the department responsible for managing the asset, the location, the asset type, the structure and detail, the acquisition costs, and its history, from acquisition to disposal. At the end of the year, physical inspections of the assets against the details of the ledger are necessary to check for completeness.

(2) Repair
If the repair of fixed assets is required, the company must check the details of the maintenance services. It must determine whether the cost of repair should be categorized as capital expenditure or as a repair expense. Typically, if the repair extends the useful life of the asset, then it can be capitalized.

(3) Depreciation

In IFRS, depreciation of fixed assets begins when it is available for use and capable of operating in the manner intended by the management. In U.S., depreciation begins when the assets are placed in service for use. Except for non-depreciable assets (e.g. land), all fixed assets are depreciated on a systematic basis over the useful life, irrespective of its earnings performance. The company adopts the depreciation method based on the accounting standard. The estimated useful life of an asset should not be changed once it has been established, unless there are new circumstances that make the original estimate inappropriate example modifying or enhancing an asset may extend its useful life (although repairs can make an asset last beyond its forecasted life the accounting life of an asset would not be extended in such a circumstance). Each part of an item of fixed assets with a cost that is significant in relation to the total cost of the item is depreciated separately in IFRS, which is permitted but not required by US-GAAP.

(4) Asset Valuation (Impairment)

The company must check the impairment of fixed assets and record the impairment loss, if necessary, based on the accounting standards.

3. Disposal of Fixed Assets

The disposal of fixed assets is done according to the appropriate procedures set by internal standards and company policies. When the disposal is carried out, verify the assets with the Fixed Asset Ledger and recognize a loss or gain on disposal. Depending on the country, the disposal may not be approved as a write-off unless the asset is processed as not reusable for tax purposes.

Internal Control Key Points

1. Estimated Risks

Major transactions related to tangible fixed assets include acquisition, sale, disposal, and depreciation. These are the expected risks for each transaction process:

4. Fixed Asset Management

【Expected Risk】

Classification	Expected Risk
Acquisition	• Posting of fictitious assets • Record another person's assets (assets that do not belong to the company) • Overestimated acquisition price
Sale	• Incomplete issuance of acquisition cost of sold assets
Disposal	• Incomplete processing of disposal
Depreciation	• Improper recognition of improper depreciation

2. Internal Control Key Points

In light of the above — mentioned risks the internal control should be carried out with the following considerations listed below.

【Pointers of Internal Control】

Classification	Internal Control
Acquisition	• Develop policies relating to fixed asset management, document the procedures for acquisition of tangible fixed asset, and ensure its compliance. • For acquisition of tangible fixed asset, the person-in-charge for purchase and another employee should perform an inspection on the fixed asset and confirm that the application for the acquisition of fixed asset has been approved by the head of the application department. • The assets that require statutory registration should be registered and recorded. The original title or deeds of the assets should be obtained and kept in a secure place. • Confirm that the purchase price of an important fixed asset is fair, based on appraisal or professional evaluation. • The approval of the Board of Directors is required for the acquisition of important fixed asset. • Confirm critical information, such as price, by validating supporting documents, including Delivery Receipts, Purchase Orders, the Fixed Asset Ledgers and the Journal Vouchers.
Sale	• Perform physical inspections to prevent incomplete recording of cost of sale. Assets that require registration and recording should be checked by comparing the details of the registration and record with those in the account record. • Perform an overall validity check on the profit and loss of sale. • Check that no buy-back condition is specified in the agreement, and confirm this with the person-in-charge and his or her counterpart.

Disposal	• Document the policies and procedures for disposal of fixed asset and ensure its compliance. • When physical disposal is required, photograph the disposal process for recording purposes. • Conduct an ocular site inspection to prevent any incomplete disposal processes. • At the time of disposal, establish communication with the Fixed Asset Ledger associate and the accounting department in a timely manner. Confirm the price and details by checking the Fixed Asset Ledger and the documents approving the disposal against the disposal documents.
Depreciation	• Ensure that the useful life and residual value of depreciation are properly applied. • Confirm that depreciation of assets acquired during the period was implemented at the time of start of utilization in business and not at the time of acquisition.
Maintenance	• Regularly conduct an ocular site inspection on tangible fixed assets and confirm that they are existing. • Conduct a periodic check of the Fixed Asset Ledger, the general ledger, and the result of inventory count. • Confirm the status of fire insurance and assets are checked for health and safety.

In addition, with the introduction of new accounting standards such as impairment accounting and asset retirement obligations, the importance of tangible fixed asset in corporate accounting has increased more than ever.

Therefore, it is necessary to establish internal rules such as fixed asset management policy and conduct a proper management of the fixed asset and the books covering their acquisition, ownership and disposal.

Tips for Good Accounting Practices!

- Cost incurred due to acquisition of assets, can be recorded as expenses in a certain situation.
- When repair is provided for fixed assets, it may be difficult to determine whether to record it as expenses or to be capitalized. The company needs to study the provisions of the accounting and tax laws of its respective country.
- Depreciation is a procedure to allocate the cost of fixed assets over its estimated useful life. In practice, it is necessary to understand the provisions of the accounting and tax laws on depreciation of its respective country.

5. Software Management

Accounting treatments of software differ in many points between accounting standards. This chapter refers to Japanese accounting standards. Each country should consider its own accounting standards in this area.

The use of Information Technology (IT) is now essential in corporate management, and a proper management of software is even more important. There are various kinds of software from internally-developed products to purchased packaged products. In accounting, software is recognized as an intangible fixed asset.

Like tangible fixed assets, intangible fixed assets have a relatively large value of acquisition and can contribute to the company's profit gains over a long period of time. Intangible fixed assets are classified under two categories: 1) Depreciable assets, which are recognized as cost through depreciation, as in the case of software and patent; and 2) Non-depreciable assets, which are not depreciated as in the case of Leaseholds, etc.

【Intangible Fixed Asset】

Classification	Asset
Depreciable assets	Software, patent rights, trademarks, utility model right, etc.
Non depreciable assets	Leasehold (Right that Lessee of the land can build a building on the land), telephone rights

Software, as an intangible asset, is managed in accordance with its own accounting standards. Software includes any programs used to perform operations on the computer, system specifications, and relevant documents such as flowcharts. Content, such as music and video, are treated separately from the software.

However, if software and contents are regarded as functionally or economically inseparable, they may be treated as one unit.

> **KEYWORD**
> - **Software**: Refers to a program or collection of computer instructions used to operate computers.
> - **Contents**: Refers to the information or materials to be processed in the program. For example, data to be processed in the database, photos and videos for imaging software and music data for music software.

Process Flow

1. Confirming Purpose of Software Production (at the time of planning of software production)

The accounting treatment for software is chosen according to the purpose of its production or use. The company must confirm the purpose of production or use at the time of software production planning during the in-house application of software production. The purpose of the software production is classified into three types as follows:

(i) Software for the purpose of order production
(ii) Software for the purpose of market sales (packaged software)
(iii) Internally used software

2. Ledger Management

The company should create a ledger for software management to properly monitor and manage the purchase, disposal, and changes of software. It needs to pay attention to the points described below. As in the case of tangible fixed assets, the company must conduct an ocular site inspection of the software and check its use on a regular basis.

(1) Version Upgrade

In some cases, the expenditure relating to the version upgrade of software falls in the category of capital expenditure. It is necessary to check the content of the software.

(2) Disposal

Disposal of software is conducted in an appropriate way to ensure that the evidence is reasonable enough to prove that the disposal was implemented.

3. Depreciation

Software is to be depreciated. The company needs to pay attention to the difference in accounting and tax methods for various countries. The capitalized value of the software and its depreciation may be processed in different ways, either for corporate accounting purposes or for tax accounting purposes.

5. Software Management

Internal Control Key points

1. Internally-Used/Developed Software

In the case of internally used or developed software, the cost is capitalized only if the use of software ensures that earnings or cost savings will certainly be produced. Accordingly, to perform an appropriate accounting treatment, the company must provide a rationale for the decision-making process leading to the conclusion that "earnings or cost savings will certainly be produced". To this end, it must confirm and clarify this in the approval document and other related documents.

In addition, when internally used/developed software is capitalized, the company must take into account the risk that software with no asset value is capitalized. Thus, there is risk that the software does not exist or its value is overestimated.

When the general purpose software is purchased from the outside, the risk of overestimating the value of the software is low. However, for example when the software is personally ordered, misconduct of resale and embezzlement may occur. Steps must be taken to prevent misconduct in the purchase of internally used software. If general-purpose software is purchased from the outside, the details of the product must be reviewed by checking the contents of its brochure.
In the case of internally used/developed software acquired by the company sourcing the system development, the purchaser must confirm the purpose and set the details of the agreement. After that, the company needs to get approval of the company supervisor. Finally, the company can execute a purchase order.

In the management of software during the holding period, the company must maintain the intangible assets ledger. It must record and manage the status of the asset's use from acquisition to disposal, since the software has an "invisible" attribute. Specifically, the company needs to cross-check the documents evidencing the new acquisition and disposal of software with the software management ledger. The details of information filled out in the forms needs verification. For confirmation of the software, a person outside the department involved in its use needs to confirm how the software is used for a specific purpose. That employee will perform regular site inspections to confirm that the software is actually used in business practices. Moreover, the company must conduct a disposal of no-longer-used assets in a timely manner.

2. Software for the Purpose of Market Sales (Packaged Software)

The cost of research and development for software used for market sales should be recorded as an expense. In order to defer the cost burden, the cost may be capitalized with the cost of other software, allocated to the production costs of other product masters, or recorded as software development in progress by treating them as order production software. These misconducts are likely to occur.

In order to prevent these misconducts, the company must establish an internal policy on research and development. It must take the following stages into consideration: calculation of the costs for each project, progress management, regular budget/result management, and the stage in the management process which recognizes an expense as the cost of research and development. After that, an approval from the head of the relevant department should be obtained.

Tips for Good Accounting Practices!

- In the case of internally used/developed software, its cost is capitalized if the use of software ensures that earnings or cost savings will certainly be produced. This is determined based on the approval document specifying the approval of software production and other related documents.
- The documents which can prove and make a prima facie showing that the start of the use of internally used/developed software, its disposal, the evidence of the completion time of product master of software for the purpose of correct market sale are required to perform proper accounting and tax processing procedures.

6. Cost Management

Cost refers to the amount that can be directly recognized and recorded in sales. For example, in the sale of one product, the cost for that specific product is recognized as cost of sales. In merchandise sales, it refers to the purchase price of the items sold. In the manufacturing industry, it refers to the manufacturing costs that are required to produce the product, such as material costs, labor costs, and overhead costs. In the service sector, it refers to service costs. In this chapter, cost management practices will be discussed.

The chapter will focus on the manufacturing costs of the manufacturing industry, especially on standard costing, which enables to control costs with comparing actual cost and standard/target cost, and analyzing the variance. For topics on purchase cost, please refer to "Chapter 2: Accounts Payable Management".

Process Flow

Cost management falls under three primary categories:
- **Cost Budgeting**: Business practice for budgeting the standard/target cost by collecting internal and external information
- **Actual Cost Computations**: Business practice for calculating the actual costs spent on the manufacturing of the product
- **Cost Variance Analysis**: Business practice for calculating the difference between budget cost and actual cost and analyzing the cause of occurrence of the difference

1. Cost Budgeting

Creating an annual cost budget is the first step in the manufacturing industry, defining the standard/target cost in the budgeting stage allows the comparison of the standard/target cost and the actual cost. This increases production efficiency and achieves cost reduction. Budgeting is one of the important processes in managing a business. The budget will be formulated/calculated by product, by factory and by expense item. When formulated/calculated, the cost budget must align with the budget proposed by the relevant departments.

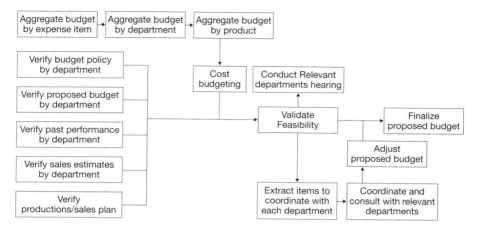

2. Actual Cost Calculation

Actual Cost Calculation achieves the following objectives:
- Preparation of financial statements: To calculate cost of sales or product cost corresponding to sales.
- Management accounting: To understand the actual value to be compared with the cost budget for the variance analysis between the standard/target cost and the actual cost.

The data relating to the actual cost is aggregated in the following order: by expense item, by department, and by product.

(1) Computation/Calculation by Expense Item

Material costs, labor costs and expenses are aggregated separately. Direct costs and indirect costs for each of the above item are also aggregated separately.

(2) Computation/Calculation by Department

Direct material costs, direct labor costs, and direct expenses are aggregated by the computation of expenses that can be directly allocated to the product. Any manufacturing overhead cost that cannot be directly allocated to the product is distributed to each production department in a pre-determined formula.

6. Cost Management

3. Computation/Calculation by Product

After the manufacturing department costs have been computed/calculated as part of department costing, the different costs of each product are aggregated through the Allocation Computation.

Computation by expense item	Computation by department	Computation by product
Direct cost		
Material cost		
Labor cost	Directly allocated to each product ⟶	
Expense		
Indirect cost		
Material cost	Distributed to each production department ⟶	Distributed to each product ⟶
Labor cost	Production department	
Expense	Auxiliary department	

4. Cost Variance Analysis

Cost Variance Analysis helps differentiate between the actual cost and the standard/target cost. Additionally, it analyzes why the differences occurred. Both favorable and unfavorable variances are considered. In addition, it is necessary to check whether or not there are non-cost items and abnormal items. In the analysis, the company must define the unit of analysis from different points of view, such as by supplier, by merchandise, by person-in-charge, and by period. Moreover, performing separate analysis for both the quantity variance and the price variance is also effective. Depending on the contents of the variance, providing feedback to each department or factory will help in budgeting and management for the following years.

Internal Control Key Points

1. Defining the Authority and Responsibility in Manufacturing Operation

The company must establish costing policies and guidelines to define the procedure and role of each operation, such as production, inspection, and inventory management. In addition, the authority and responsibility should be clarified to ensure that every aspect of the operation is efficiently managed.

2. Appropriateness of Estimated Items

Since there are estimated items such as expected purchase price for material and standard capacity, the company needs to ensure the accuracy of the figure which will become the basis for costing. The supervisor needs to provide an appropriate approval of the estimated items.

3. Validity of Aggregation Procedures

The company must check whether the cost aggregation and the cost variance are appropriately processed and reflected in the accounting records. Specifically, it is important that those cost aggregation and cost variances are checked by a second party who is not involved in the process and approved by the supervisor.

 Tips for Good Accounting Practices!

- Understand the special terms of cost calculation, and become familiar with the calculation procedure.
- Proper execution of cost variance analysis provides useful data for cost management.
- To achieve accuracy and efficiency, the process should be automated. Costing system should be implemented and developed with caution.

7. Expense Management

To increase revenue, the company must make a payment of expenses. This is required for tracking sales activities and maintaining the business management. Expense is a generic term for these costs. This chapter will discuss topics on practices of expense management.

Process Flow

1. Budget
(1) Preparation of Annual Budget
A company needs to plan which departments and items should funds get allocated. The plan ensures effective and efficient use of its limited funds. This expense plan is made in the form of a budget plan.

(2) Comparison of Budget and Actual
Developing a budget plan is not enough to perform expense management. A company needs to know how much expense was incurred with reference to its budget. Effective expense management can be performed by conducting business activities based on the budget, comparing it with the resulting actual value, and analyzing the variance.

2. Expense Processing
(1) Ordinary Expense Processing
There are three patterns of incurring expenses:
(i) The accounting department pays directly to an external party by cash, wire transfer or other means at the request of other departments based on approved purchase requisitions/orders and matched to supplier invoices
(ii) If a staff makes an advance payment, the accounting department reimburses him or her at a later date.
(iii) An estimated amount of money is given in advance to a staff member. After the staff has spent it, the excess or deficiency of the amount is settled at a later date.

Number (i) is the most common pattern. No matter which pattern is used, the expenses should be processed in accordance with company policy. After the expenses are paid, the company should prepare supporting documents including processing slips, in a timely manner.

3. Settlement/Payment
(1) Cash Advance
Verify the Cash Advance supporting documents with the Request for Cash Advance Form before approving any liquidation or reimbursement. Post the transfer to the appropriate account.

(2) Margin Settlement
Margin settlement is used to settle the difference between the cash advance amount and the actual amount. A voucher to process the difference is prepared.

Internal Control Key Points

1. Payroll Expenses
(1) Preparation of an Employee Master File
The Human Resource Department should manage individual personnel records by preparing and compiling a personnel database (Employee Master File). Depending on the country, certain personnel information is required to be collected by law.
The individual personnel records included in the Employee Master File are as follows:
(i) Basic information about the staff, such as birth certificate, resume and information received at the time of recruitment;
(ii) Personnel records at the company, such as employment contract, payroll history, promotion, transfer; and
(iii) Payroll and timekeeping records, such as basic information for payroll computation, vacation leave, sick leave and AWOL (absence without leave). Timekeeping information is important in some countries. It is required by law to monetize the unconsumed leaves. For the above reason, the supervisor must approve and make a periodic review of the records. Basic information for payroll computation is updated in a timely manner. The details must be verified by

a second party other than the person in charge. Strict confidentiality is required in managing this master file.

(2) Prepare Payroll Computation Table
The timesheet is the source of payroll computation. It is required to be approved by the supervisor. Independent personnel other than the personnel who prepared the timesheet, must re-compute and approve the payroll computation table.

(3) Disburse Payroll
Fraud related to payment of payroll is often carried out by several means including the creation of fictitious payees, non-cancellation of retirees, padding of the total amount, etc. To prevent these frauds, the company must segregate the duty of the payroll and fund disbursement personnel.

(4) Recording of Payroll etc.
The company must segregate the duty of the person processing the payment (disbursement of the actual salary) and that of the person posting. In many case in small organizations, the person responsible for payroll computation is also in charge of voucher preparation and posting. In this case, the voucher must be approved by the supervisor.

2. Operating Expenses
(1) Approval of the Supervisor
The department where expenses are incurred is required to complete the approval procedures for the expense. To process an expense exceeding a certain amount or for a certain type of expense, company policy may require a special approval process. Every approval should comply with the Authority Matrix and done in accordance with the approval policy stated in the Company Policy.

(2) Documentation of Job Description and Segregation of Duty
The Job Description documents the authority, duty and responsibility of each staff member. The segregation of duties for certain jobs is recommended in order to implement stronger internal control. For example, the expense task can be divided into the three types of processes: accruing, payment and recording. Defining the scope of "who can and who should do what" is also strongly recommended.

(3) Advertising Expenses

The cost-effectiveness of some expenses, such as advertising expenses, are difficult to understand due to the nature of the expense. Such expenses can be greater than expected. To examine the effect of spending in advance, a company must create a plan and obtain an approval from the authorized personnel of the company.

(4) Entertainment Expenses

Before spending, a company needs to check whether or not the expense falls within the scope of provision of benefits without charge. In addition, unaccounted-for expenditure should be checked whether it should bear the spending. A company must obtain an approval from authorized personnel of the company.

(5) Donation

The company should consider whether it should bear the spending. A company must obtain an approval from authorized personnel of the company.

 Tips for Good Accounting Practices!

- Since the success of cost management greatly affects the profit and loss of the company, the company should reduce wasteful spending and manage expenses.
- Since cost management includes a lot of items subject to tax assessment, it is important to perform accounting in consideration of the tax risks.

8. Monthly Performance Management

The Monthly Performance Management refers to the process of checking (SEE) the actual results (DO) against the plan developed using medium-term planning, long-term planning and the annual budget (PLAN). The typical approach is a monthly closing of accounting books.

The monthly closing of accounting books refers to closing of accounts to provide useful financial information for business management. This is in addition to the closing to be performed at the end of the year.

The annual closing of accounting books is required to be performed according to the laws and regulations of the respective country. The monthly closing of accounts is not required by law to be performed but they are done for management account purposes. This important closing process provides basic information for the quarterly results and annual accounting. The monthly closing of accounts is performed for the following purposes.

【Purposes of Monthly Closing of Accounts】

• To grasp the situation of management at an early stage so to take prompt measures for untoward incidences.
• To perform monitoring and progress management by setting a target on the sales, operating income and net income of the annual plan (medium-term and long-term planning management and annual budget management).
• To predict sales and profit for the annual report at an early stage, and make a highly reliable estimate of results.
• To perform a more accurate annual closing of accounts by ensuring a monthly processing of the books.

Among other things, the primary concern for the management, in terms of comparison with the plan, is the monthly closing of accounts. The information about the closing of accounts is expected to be provided to the management as soon as possible. To do this, the accounting and finance departments are requested to provide a monthly closing and variance analysis of budget and performance at the earliest possible date.

Process Flow

The flow of Monthly Performance Management is as follows.

1. Monthly Closing Adjustment

The company must check the balances of various accounts and perform closing adjustments in order to match the business activity to financial activity within a given period (usually monthly) normally referred to as the accruals concept. The accrual concept in accounting means that expenses and revenues are recorded in the period they occur, whether or not cash is involved. The closing adjustment includes recognition of deferred income, (e.g., suspense accounts such as suspense receipts) and the recording of accrued expenses. (e.g., recognition of depreciation, provision of various allowances, bonuses, labor, insurance premiums, damage insurance, and other expenses incurred during the month but not yet recognized.) The computation method must be predetermined and items need to be recorded.

When foreign exchange rates and interest rates are required for monthly closing, the company must predetermine what rates are used for monthly closing. It can be monthly average rate, rate of the last day of the month, etc. according to the applicable accounting standards.

8. Monthly Performance Management

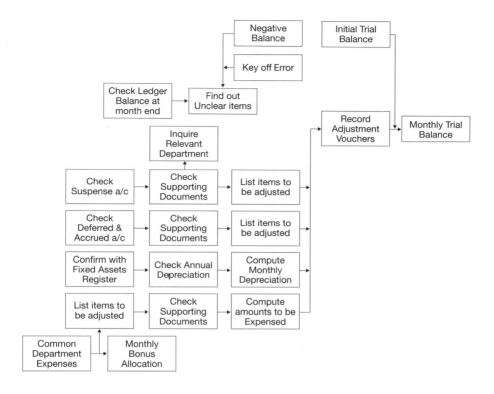

2. Monthly Performance Verification

The company must review the details of the monthly closing and report the results to the management.

The performance report, based on monthly closing, is aimed to quickly understand the conditions and issues of the operation. The report reviews documents including a comparison and analysis of the budget (or the prior year performance) against the actual performance. Based on the report results, the company must implement measures to achieve the company objective. Therefore, this report is required to provide accurate and prompt information.

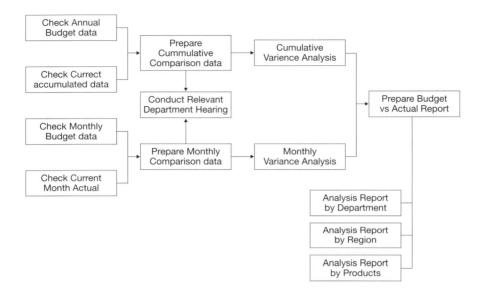

3. Budget Review

Significant discrepancies in the monthly budget can alter the result of the budget performance analysis. If so, the expected results from the annual budget are likely to change dramatically. It will be necessary to adjust and modify the annual budget set forth at the beginning of the year, with reference to the actual results. The budget may be modified on a quarterly basis or on a half-year basis, depending on the deviation range of projection. Generally, the original budget is modified in a set period of time of the first half year and becomes a re-forecast to the end of the annual financial period.

8. Monthly Performance Management

 Tips for Good Accounting Practices!

- Monthly closing is to be carried out to make a report for the company's management. This closing is required to be performed accurately and promptly.
- There is no fixed form for a monthly closing document (although some countries recommend standard formats). The company must review and determine the contents of the report to meet its needs. Afterwards, the management can reach the right decision on its operations and take prompt measure, essentially it is a feedback mechanism for the business like PDCA (Plan Do Check Act)
- Depending on the size of the company, it is not necessary to show numbers in the exact amount of the currency. Sometimes, it is more practical to report using bigger amounts of one thousand (1,000) or one million (1,000,000), whichever is appropriate.

9. Financial Closing Process

The purpose of Financial Closing is to provide the financial reporting to stakeholders such as shareholders, investors and others. Therefore, the final goal of Financial Closing is to create various closing documents, such as financial statements, in accordance with the accounting standards. Additionally, it aims to complete the legal approval process of the Board of Directors in the General Meeting of Shareholders Meeting, etc., after auditing. In other words, it is very important to obtain legal approval.

Process Flow

Usually the conversion of monthly management financial performance into annual statutory financial reporting is based on local GAAP and or International GAAP. The workflow is illustrated in the flowchart below.

| Preparations in Advance | Financial Closing Process | Reporting to Directors (Officers) and Auditing | Approval Procedures at the General Meeting of Shareholders |

1. Preparations in Advance
(1) Developing the Closing Policy

The first step is to develop a closing policy that management, including the CFO, will approve. Closing policy is roughly divided into two types of policy: accounting policy and policy on profit and dividend.

A. Accounting Policy

The company must adopt the appropriate local or international accounting standard and confirm the impact of the local tax law on the accounting practices. If the accounting method needs to be changed, the company should consult with their auditors and agreed upon the change. Then, the new accounting method is applied.

B. Policy on Profit and Dividend

The information on how much final profit will be recognized in the closing of the current fiscal year and how much dividend will be paid to shareholders is the primary concern of top management. Before starting the work of the annual accounting, the company needs to create a prediction of financial results, calculate profit projections and earnings available for dividends, and report the information to the top management.

(2) Developing the Closing Schedule

It is necessary to develop a closing schedule that takes into account the date of the General Meeting of Shareholders and the deadline set out by the Parent Company. When developing a closing schedule the company is required to develop a long enough schedule for the Financial Closing Process. The schedule must take into account a closing schedule for the internal system. Generally, the success of closing depends on the appropriate arrangement for closing. This process is very important in annual accounting practice.

(3) Assigning of Personnel In-charge of Account Closing

The company must assign personnel who will be in-charge of the closing in accordance with the above-mentioned closing schedule. It must take into account each person's capacity and a future plan for human resource development.

It should be noted that, if the person in charge has less experience, the supervisor must review his or her work and support him or her more closely.

(4) Confirmation and Review of Common Matters

In financial closing, it is necessary to confirm and review common matters as a prerequisite. Specifically, the following matters need to be reviewed: 1) Exchange rate at closing date and for the period; 2) Criteria for recording provisions; 3) Evaluation criteria of assets; 4) Allocation criteria of common expenses; and 5) Others.

(5) Internal Notification and Holding a Briefing Session

When the advance preparation has been completed, the company must give an internal notification of the annual closing to each department, and hold a briefing session as necessary. It is also necessary to give an internal notification with the name of the director in charge of accounting and finance or the CFO to ensure that the closing policy is maintained throughout the company from accounting level to higher levels.

2. Financial Closing Procedures
(1) Supporting Relevant Departments
The company needs to support each department in accounting procedures including the consultation on the accounting treatment. This ensures that each department can complete the closing procedures on a timely basis according to the closing schedule.

(2) Establishment of Sales
In accordance with the adopted recognition criteria for sales, the company needs to determine the sales of the current period. There are many companies that have adopted the accounting method called sales on dispatch to record sales at the time of product coming out of the gate of the factory. There are many other accounting standards, such as delivery basis, customers' acceptance criteria, percentage of completion, and completed-contract basis. Please also refer to the Chapter 1. Accounts Receivable Management. It is highly recommended to choose an accounting standard that suits the situation of trading and to comply with the provisions of the accounting rules and regulations.

The company must check whether the sales recorded before and after the end of term are properly recognized with reference to the revenue recognition standard adopted by the company. Furthermore, it must check if there is an indication of channel stuffing or fictitious sales giving priority to profit were performed. This is done by cross-checking the sales book and supporting documents. If there are any questions or concerns, please confirm and clarify them with the supervisor.

(3) Establishment of Cost
After the sales have been established, the company must confirm that costs are correctly recorded in accordance with the calculation criteria of cost of sales. In particular, it is important to understand the actual amount of inventory/stock through physical inventory, and establish the costs by evaluating the year-end inventories. Please also refer to the Chapter 3. Inventory Management and 6. Cost Management.

(4) Allocation of Common Expenses
Common expenses or indirect expenses are costs which do not have a clear corresponding relationship with sales, such as the expenses incurred in the administrative division of the factory. Normally, such common expenses are allocated to costs based on certain allocation criteria. The person in charge must perform proper

calculations and determine the cost of sales. Please also refer to the Chapter 6. Cost management.

(5) Closing Adjustments

In the annual closing, there are special adjustment procedures called closing adjustments. The examples of closing adjustments are described as follows.

(i) Adjustment of suspense account

Suspense accounts refer to any accounts, such as suspense payments and suspense receipt, temporarily used without being recorded in the original account for some reasons, such as unknown contents or unclear accounting processing. Suspense accounts may cumulatively increase if proper care is not taken. As a result, it may require a long time to adjust them. Therefore, it is highly recommended to thoroughly review the contents on a monthly basis and transfer them to the proper account.

(ii) Calculation of deferred and accrued accounts

This is matching sales and costs to the activity of the financial period being reported. Deferred and accrued accounts refer to accounts used for adjusting the period of account. This is used to perform an appropriate profit and loss calculation for a certain period of time. There are several types of accounts, such as prepaid expenses, accrued expenses, accrued income and unearned income. If they are processed on a cash basis during the year, it is necessary to perform the procedures for adjusting to the accrual basis of accounting at the year-end.

Method of Calculating Deferred and Accrued Accounts

In general there are two types of method of calculating deferred and accrued accounts: (i) the method of keeping accounts on a cash basis during the period and recognizing them in the closing, and (ii) the method of recognizing items during the period and adjusting them from time to time after confirmation of payment and income.

Method (i) is advantageous because the work process is simple, but it is disadvantageous because it creates a large variance in the profit and loss in the closing month. On the other hand, the method (ii) is advantageous because the profit and loss are equalized and accounting processing of accounts receivable and accounts payable can be performed properly. However, it is disadvantageous because the accounting processing is complicated.

Some of the accounting packages available nowadays provide smooth processing functions incorporating the method (ii) including the concepts: AR (Accounts Receivable: Accounts Receivable module) and AP (Accounts Payable: Accounts Payable module). Thus, the method (ii) becoming a major accounting processing method.

(iii) Adjusting long-term and short-term receivables and payables

To list receivables and payables on the balance sheet need to be classified as current assets, current liabilities, fixed assets and long-term liabilities. It is necessary to extract information from the management ledger and management system and perform the transfer processing.

KEYWORD

For the purpose of accounting, it is necessary to determine whether receivables or payables are long-term or short-term, according to the following criteria:

- **Operating Cycle Criteria**: Assets and liabilities converted to cash or revenue and expense in the normal operating cycle (business cycle) are classified as short-term (current assets or current liabilities). Inventories and accounts receivable / accounts payable generated by operating activities are assets and liabilities in the operating cycle, and therefore they should be classified as current assets (or current liabilities), even if the settlement is made in more than one year.
- **One Year Rule (Accounting Period)**: When the due date of the receivables and liabilities occurs within one year from the day following the closing date, they are classified as short-term (current assets or current liabilities), and when the due date of the receivables and liabilities occurs after more than one year, they are classified as long-term (investments and other assets or long-term liabilities).

9. Financial Closing Process

(iv) Account scrutiny

It is necessary to cross-check the assets with the evidential documents such as an auxiliary book and certificates of deposit balance and scrutinize whether or not the balance of the account is correct. If there is anything unclear in the content, you need to investigate on the details by reviewing individual slips or evidential documents. The failure to make payment related to withholding tax deposits, etc. will be discovered through this procedure as well.

In accounting practice, if an accounts breakdown table is prepared together with this procedure, the accounting processing will be performed more efficiently.

(v) Recording of various provisions

It is necessary to make an estimate calculation of the accounts such as allowance for doubtful accounts, allowance for retirement benefits, and reserve or provision for bonuses with reference to the basis for recording various provisions. First of all, before calculating the provisions and others, you need to temporarily fix the amount of the receivable covered for allowance for doubtful accounts, the amount of the bonus covered for bonus allowance, etc.

If you use outside services for any element required for financial closing such as an estimate calculation of allowance for retirement benefits held by trust company (e. g. trust bank or other financial institutions), you must make sure the report is built into the financial closing process.

(vi) Evaluation and impairment test of assets

The assets such as particular securities, real estate and others require evaluation and possible impairment. It is necessary to obtain the information of market value of the asset and other relevant information in accordance with the company's criteria of evaluation and impairment test.

(6) Calculation of Tax Effect such as Income Taxes

After the pre-tax net income is finalized, it is necessary to calculate the taxable income and the corporate income tax. If these calculations are entrusted to an external accounting firm, you must check the schedule and the provided materials in advance and obtain them in a timely manner.

(7) Finalizing Closing Numerical Value

As described above, after the provision of corporate income tax, etc. has been finalized, the current after tax net income is calculated, and then the final Trial Balance

is prepared. The use of the information obtained through these procedures allows you to finalize a balance sheet, an income statement, and a statement of changes in stockholders' equity. (A balance sheet, an income statement and a statement of changes in stockholders' equity, along with separate notes to the financial statements and supplementary schedules, are legally finalized through the approval of the Board of Directors and the general shareholders' meeting).
In the UK this process would be classed as the Statutory Accounts Package.

(8) Confirmation of Subsequent Events

Subsequent events refer to the significant accounting events which occur during the period from the day after the closing date to the audit report that affect the financial condition and operating results of the company. You need to check with the law firm before the disclosure date whether such event has occurred and treat them as a disclosure item, if necessary.

3. Reporting to Directors and Preparation of Audit
(1) Closing Analysis

After the closing of numerical value has been finalized, you will analyze the contents of the financial results of the current period. The documents should be created as requested by the management, but in general it is necessary to conduct a comparative analysis of the numerical values of the current year and the previous year, a comparative analysis of the budget or the projections, and a content analysis of abnormal values, etc. These analyses are also important to prevent major errors in closing process.

(2) Preparation of Audit Based on Local GAAP and or International GAAP

In a company with the auditors (external and Board of Corporate Auditors), the following documents must be provided to the auditors, as prescribed by the Parent Company.
- (i) **Financial statements** (Stand-alone balance sheet, income statement, statement of changes in stockholders' equity, and separate notes to the financial statements) and supplementary schedules.
- (ii) **Consolidated financial statements** (consolidated balance sheet, consolidated income statement, consolidated statement of changes in stockholders' equity,

and notes to consolidated financial statements)

(iii) Business report and supplementary schedules
In addition, Japanese company with the external auditor (Large companies with a capital of 500 million yen or more or with a total debt of 20 billion yen or more are obliged to have an external auditor), the above-mentioned documents with the exception of the business report and supplementary schedules must be audited by the external auditor.

(3) Preparation of Audit
It is necessary to organize and arrange the audit schedule, audit items, and documents to be submitted with auditors for advance preparation.

(4) Organizing and Managing the Audit
Normally, the accounting department organizes and manages the audit. The internal audit manager or a person in similar position, who acts as an intermediary between the responsible department and internal/external auditors, must convey their inquiries to the relevant departments accurately and make appropriate arrangements for a smooth audit.

(5) Addressing Errors, Omissions and Misstatement (Audit Findings)
You need to take measures for the errors, omissions and misstatements detected through the audit, and consult with the auditors. These detected matters/audit findings should be reported to the management, and if nessesary, the relevant information entered in the books and the financial statements should be adjusted.

(6) Obtaining the Audit Report
In the final stage of the audit, you need to obtain audit reports from the external auditors. In the audit report made by the external auditors, any of the following auditor's opinion may be issued: 1) unqualified; 2) qualified; 3) adverse; and 4) disclaimer. Generally, an audit report is in principle submitted with unqualified opinion. This means that the financial statements of the company are presented fairly in all material aspects in accordance with the appropriate accounting standard. To do this, as described in (5) you need to consult with the auditors about the important matters that have been discovered through the audit, and if necessary, report

them to the top management, and then modify/adjust the financial statements based on the auditors' findings, and obtain the approval.

(7) Preparation of the Board of Directors Agenda Materials and Approval of the Board of Directors

Under the Companies Act in Japan, a company with external auditors or board of corporate auditors, after being audited by auditors, the financial statements (balance sheet, income statement, statement of changes stockholders' equity, and notes to the financial statements), the business report and their supplementary schedules must be approved by the Board of Directors.

4. Preparation for the General Meeting of Shareholders (In Case of Japan)
(1) Approval of Financial Statements, etc.

The Companies Act prescribes that the financial statements, etc. shall, in principle, be finalized by approved resolution of the general shareholders' meeting.

However, in the case of a company with external auditors, if the financial reporting meets the following requirements: (i) the external auditor expresses an unqualified opinion in his/her report; and (ii) there is no opinion in the audit reports by auditors or board of auditors which concludes that the audit methods and results provided by the external auditor are not reasonable, and (iii) there are no other negative comments, the financial statements are finalized upon the approved resolution of the Board of Directors and treated as reporting matters at the General Meeting of Shareholders.

(2) Appropriation of Surplus

The Companies Act intends to impose various regulations on the calculation performed by the company and its main purpose is to carry out appropriation of its surplus properly. Under the current Companies Act, the company can declare dividends at any time and any number of times, but the maximum amount of dividend that can be paid (distributable amount) is defined in detail in the Companies Act, and therefore confirmation of the distributable amount must be carefully performed according to the calculation method stipulated by law.

After the financial statements, etc. have been finalized through the statutory procedures, the date of dividends declaration and payment will be approved through a Board Resolution at the general meeting of shareholders.

9. Financial Closing Process

In a Board Resolution, it is important to note the record date of stockholders. Such record date will determine who are entitled for the dividends. It is necessary to specify the amount of dividends in notes on a statement of changes in net assets according to the provisions of the Companies Act.

Internal Control Key Points

With respect to closing procedures, it is effective to check the items listed in the table below.

【Closing Checklist】

Account Title	Method	Contents or purposes
All accounts	Creating the previous fiscal year comparison table	• Review and analyze the reason of increase/decrease
		• Find errors in account treatment
	Creating monthly movement table	• Prepare financial statement notes and tax return
		• Find errors in account treatment
Cash/Deposit	Physical inspection- cash count and bank confirmation	• Finalize the amount to be recorded in the balance sheet
Accounts receivable	Balance confirmation with a customer	• Finalize the amount to be recorded in the balance sheet
		• Prevent and detect fraud
	Aging	• Check classification of balance sheet • Confirm the necessity for recording allowance for doubtful accounts (bad debt)
Securities	Verify with Certificate of Balance	• Prevent and detect fraud
Notes receivable	Physical inspection	• Finalize the amount to be recorded in the balance sheet
		• Prevent and detect fraud
	Checking bill maturities	• Check classification of balance sheet
		• Credit management

Suspense accounts such as suspense payment, suspense receipt	Creating a detailed statement by account	• Check the account title on balance sheet • Prevent and detect fraud
Inventory	Physical inventory	• Finalize the amount to be recorded in the balance sheet
		• Confirm the processing status of returned goods, etc.
		• Detect defective and obsolete goods
	Prepare account detailed statement	• Find errors in account treatment
		• Confirm the presence or absence of excess/short stock
Fixed asset	Physical inspection	• Check existence, completeness and physical condition
		• Confirm recording loss on disposal, etc.
	Prepare account details/schedules	• Check depreciation cost
		• Prepare supplementary schedules notes etc.
Accounts payable, notes payable	Verify the account balance with transaction counterpart	• Finalize the amount to be recorded in the balance sheet
		• Prevent and detect fraud
	Prepare the account details/schedules	• Confirm outstanding accounts payable
Other assets and liabilities	Prepare the account details/schedules	• Find errors in account treatment
		• Check the account title on balance sheet
Sales and purchasing	Prepare Historical Performance Report (monthly comparison)	• Confirm the validity of the processing of sales and returned goods, etc. near year-end
		• Check correspondence of sales and cost
Expense	Prepare Historical Performance Report (monthly comparison)	• Investigate the cause of increased or decreased items
		• Find errors in account treatment
Other	Check Contract	• Check whether transactions and account processing are performed according to the contract
		• Check the validity of contract

Tips for Good Accounting Practices!

- The purpose of monthly closing of books of accounts is to address the needs of internal user within the company, while the purpose of annual closing is to address the needs for both internal and external users of the financial reports. For this reason, the procedures and the forms of financial statements, etc. are prescribed by law. The closing procedures (closing policy), development of closing schedule, and assignment of duties, etc. must be prepared to perform the closing smoothly.

10. Annual Budget Management

Budget is the numerical description of the specific goals of a company for a given year. Budget is developed by translating the business forecast into a shorter-term plan with individual business operations. The medium and long-term plans are created based on the management philosophy of the company.

Budget management refers to the management approach in controlling the operations and activities of the company to achieve the budget targets set at the beginning of the year or the beginning of fiscal operations. Budget management is one of the first steps used to grow and to develop the company. The budget management goes through the same steps as the medium and long-term planning process.

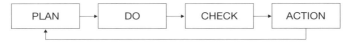

The steps for budget management are as follows: First, develop a budget (PLAN). Second, carry out the business operations (DO). Third, manage the operations (CHECK). Finally, analyze the difference between the budget and actual results and resolve the problems (ACTION). If any changes occur, the company should adjust the budget as soon as possible. They should also provide feedback for the budget of the following year.

Process Flow

1. Developing Budget Management Policy

First of all, management instructs each department to set up its sales target, expense forecast, and profit target. This instruction intends to provide targets based on the medium and long-term plan. Therefore, after cross-checking the economic environment and the market trends used as the basis for the medium and long-term plan, the budgeting department (e.g., The Budget Committee, Planning Department,

10. Annual Budget Management

Accounting Department, etc.) needs to notify and explain the budget to each department. In this case, it is also necessary to clarify the budget policy and developing schedule.

2. Developing Budget by Department

Next, every department develops a budget for each item, taking into account the feasibility of achieving the target. The main items are sales budget, production cost budget, capital investment budget, staffing budget, fund budget, etc. Since the items may be utilized across departments, each department needs to coordinate with the relevant departments. In addition, the budgeting department helps each department create an appropriate budget by providing guidance and support.

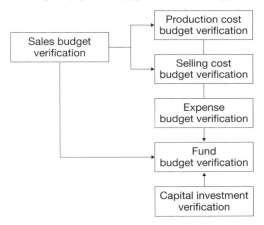

3. Finalizing Annual Budget

At this stage, the budgets that have been submitted by each department are compiled. The overall budget is completed. A budget for the entire company (company-wide annual budget) is created based on this information. This step will be conducted mainly by the budgeting department. In compiling the budget, consistency with the medium and long-term plan, consistency between the departments and other matters should be considered carefully. If required, timely revisions to the budget can be made. Once coordination with stakeholders has been completed, the approval of the management should be obtained. Such finalized budgets are notified and explained to each department and employees. Full implementation of the budget depends on the proper understanding of each department and all employees at every level.

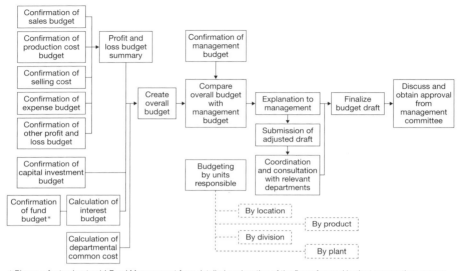

*Please refer to chapter 14 Fund Management for a detailed explanation of the flow of annual budget preparation process

Budget Management Key Points

1. Significance of Budgeting

Developing the medium and long-term plan is not sufficient to achieve the goals, therefore, the annual budget is required. Specifically, the significances are described as follows:

(1) Goal Setting

The goals listed in the medium and long-term plans cover the period of at least three to five years. In budgeting, a short-term goal for the next one year is setup. Setting specific goals are possible. Short-term plans are the first step to achieve the performance goals.

(2) Business Administration

A more concrete budget will result in clear and more definite numerical targets. Using the budget based on the numerical targets, the entire company can be

10. Annual Budget Management

effectively controlled. In other words, the company can improve its management process by using progress management and comparing the budget and actual results. As in the process of medium and long-term planning, the set of budget targets helps facilitate communication between the company's management and its employees. This communication can help its employees to achieve their goals and enhance their motivation.

2. Work Flow of Budgeting

1	Budgeting policy
2	Setting, adjustment and decision of each budget item
3	Developing overall budget
4	Do implementation
5	Analysis of variance between budget and actual results
6	Consider action plans and measures

3. Setting Method

The three methods for budget setting are described in the table below.

Method	Description	Advantages	Disadvantages
Top-down method	• This method reflects the management's decision. The top management sets the objectives for the company and translates them into concrete goals for the middle management and operational level employees to achieve.	• Because decision making and budgeting are done almost at the same time, a quick budget setting can be expected. • Because the budget is broken down by the management, it is possible to set a proportioned budget as a whole.	• There is a possibility that the management may set an unrealistic budget that does not take the actual situation into consideration. • Sometimes, since the budget does not consider the viewpoint of the employees, the employees may be less motivated to achieve their goals. • Sometimes, since the employees were not involved enough in preparation of the budget, they might not accept ownership of achieving it.

Bottom-up method	• This method recognizes the inputs from employees at the operational level. In other words, it is intended to build up from the bottom and integrates individual budgets at each level into a company-wide budget.	• Since the person in charge who understands the situation sets the budget, the department can set a more realistic budget. • As the budget recognizes the inputs from employee, they are more motivated to achieve their goals.	As the budget is built up from the bottom, there is a risk that the budget setting would be too time-consuming. • Sometimes, the budget is set based on the employees' past experiences and are less goal-oriented. Thus, the employees may set budgets that are easy to achieve. • When the integration work is not well done, the budget tends to lack the overall balance.
Compromise method	• This method combines both of the previous methods. In other words, after the company sets its budget policy through the management decision-making process, each department develops a budget and integrates them into a whole.	• Because the budget reflects the intentions of the management and each department, it will be well-balanced.	The management has to pass down the budget policy to each department, who will set the budget from bottom up and integrates them into a finalized budget. Thus, there is a risk that the budgeting would be too time-consuming. • Friction can occur if the coordination between management and each department does not go well.

4. Responsibility of Budgeting

The coordination and adjustment of the budget between departments are the responsibilities of either the planning department, budget committee, or the accounting department. Budgeting mainly involves numerical processes. For budgeting work, the department in charge of the numerical processes plays a central role.

The assigned department provides information for decision making on the budgeting policy to the top management. Based on top management's instructions regarding the budgeting policy, it requests each department to perform the budgeting and adjusts the budgets gathered from those departments.

When the budget has been executed, the department responsible performs an analysis of variances between the budget and actual results and submits the report of variance analysis to the management.

5. Budget Period

The budget period should be determined depending on the actual situation of the company in terms of the significance of the budget. The Annual Budget usually covers a period of one year. Most of the companies use a one year period and take into account the comparison with annual closing, frequency of budgeting, time and effort. With the spread of budget management systems and the development of IT, some companies have used a combination of either a semi-annual budget, a quarterly budget, or a monthly budget.

6. Unit of Budget

One of the questions regarding budgeting is about which of the departments should make a budget. The unit of budget depends on the scope of management. The unit for budgeting is used to set a target value and to manage the execution of the budget. It is also used to control the budget. Specifically, the units such as department, section, project, property and/or accounts are listed.

7. Relationship with the Medium and Long-term Planning

The annual budget has a more concrete and detailed content derived from the medium and long-term plan. In other words, the budget is an execution plan for the medium and long-term strategic plan. In the budget setting, it must maintain consistency with the medium and long-term plan.

8. System of Budget

The system of the budget depends on the significance of budget setting and the actual situation of the company. One of the examples appears below.

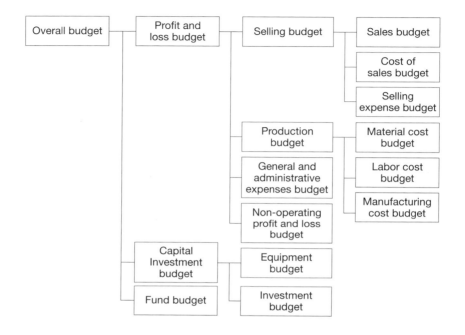

9. Selling Budget
(1) Sales Budget
In many cases, some of the contents of the sales budget are determined in details of the sales plan, including the medium and long-term sales plan. The sales plan by product and by customer is created by each department and compiled. It should consist of sales quantity and sales price details.

The company creates the sales budget by taking into account general economic conditions, the trends of competitors, customer forecasts and other factors that may affect the sales forecast together with the previous year sales volume. The sales budget should also reflect special factors that occur during the current year. The method of calculating the annual sales by creating a monthly base is ideal. In this case, the seasonal variation factor should also be taken into account.

(2) Cost of Sales Budget
It is important that the cost of sales budget corresponds to the sales budget. It is necessary to create the cost of sales budget by product and by customer. If the cost

of sales budget is created based on sales volume, the sales volumes must maintain consistency with the cost of sales. Also, if they have a certain percentage relationship to the sales prices, the company can adopt the cost ratio calculation method. The cost of sales budget should not exceed the sales budget.

(3) Selling Expense Budget
Selling expenses relate proportionally to sales. These include shipping costs, sales commissions, and other variable expenses that directly related with sales. Selling expense budget corresponds to the sales budget. If the sales volume increases, normally the shipping cost will increase. Therefore, the company must maintain a certain consistency between the selling expense budget and the sales budget. Some expenses which are not variable with sales such as advertising expenses are also included in the selling expense budget. In this case, the company makes a roll-up calculation by product. It must take into account the sales plan and the trend of past spending. In some companies, the advertising budget is developed based on the sales ratio representing the percentage of sales.

10. Production Budget
Based on the medium and long-term production plan, the company will set the budget by considering its production capacity. Standard costing is often used to make the production budget. Any plans for cost reduction measures should be reflected in the production budget.

(1) Material Cost Budget
Production forecast is set in reference to sales volume. It is necessary to pay attention to its relationship with the sales budget. The material cost budget must be consistent with the production plan. For each type of material, the department calculates the material cost budget. The material cost budget remains as inventory at the end of the period, if it is relatively greater to the growth of sales volume.

The inventory at the beginning and the end of the period of the prior year are important in determining the material cost budget. The company must understand the inventory turnover rate based on previous year experience.

(2) Labor Cost Budget
The labor cost budget is divided into two classifications: (1) occupation, such as

technician, supervisor and worker; and (2) employment status, such as full-time and part-time.

For the items that occur as a fixed cost, regardless of the production volume, the monthly budgeted salary can be determine by multiplying the average salary of employees (based on previous year or projected amount) by the actual or projected head count for the current year budget.

For items that occur as variable costs depending on production volume and working hours, like part-time jobs, the company needs to obtain the annual average unit salary. This is calculated by dividing the total amount obtained by summing up "working hours × hourly rate" by the number of personnel. Afterwards, calculate the budget by multiplying it by the number of people. The budget may be obtained by multiplying the wage per working hour by total working hours. The company must define the components of budget according to the type of occurrence then calculate the budget. The calculation for the annual average salary per person needs to take into account a base increase including periodic pay raise. A roll-up calculation for individuals and summing them up is another method to calculate the budget. The type of computation used for the calculation of the labor cost budget always depends on the complexity of operation and the costing method adopted by different companies.

In actual practice, there is no definite rule in setting up the labor cost budget. The important consideration is that the budgeted labor cost should estimate the actual cost.

(3) Manufacturing Cost Budget

Like the material costs budget, manufacturing cost budget occurs in proportion to the planned production volume. The company must determine the ratio of manufacturing cost budget with the projected sales.

Expenses, other than outsourcing processing costs, need to be divided into two groups: 1) variable costs; and 2) fixed costs.

Variable cost ratio is based on the changes in the economic environment and information from the previous years. Items which generate in proportion to the capacity utilization, such as power costs and fuel costs, are calculated based on the variable cost rate for each account.

Fixed costs, including depreciation and rent expenses occur regardless of the capacity utilization. They need to be set as a budget item according to the nature of each expense. For example, a mostly fixed amount occurs in depreciation for each period.

New acquisitions and the sale of assets are added or subtracted from the budget. The manufacturing cost budget must maintain consistency with the equipment plan.

> **KEYWORD**
> - **Capacity Utilization**: It refers to the degree of utilization of production equipment capacity. (e.g., operating time of machinery and equipment, direct working time, production volume, etc.)

11. General Administrative Expenses Budget

General administrative costs are basically treated as fixed costs. They are classified as two types of item: average annual salary per person and the number of people. The budget is set by multiplying the average annual salary by the actual or projected head count. Annual average salary per person should include the anticipated pay increases. A roll-up calculation for individuals is another method to calculate the budget. The number of people required for the personnel plan in the medium term and long-term plan may not be sufficient. In that case, the company must anticipate the costs associated with the recruitment, education, and expenses for transfers and relocations.

Other than labor costs, most of expenses occur as fixed costs. The company needs to calculate the budget in consideration of the circumstances of the previous year for each account. When the budget is calculated on the basis of the previous year's trend, there is a tendency to develop the budget in a conservative way and allocate more expenses than required. A reference frame for total expenses must be assigned to each department and a budget for cost reduction must be set.

12. Non-Operating Profit and Loss Budget
(1) Finance-Related Revenue

Interest and dividend income are calculated based on expected interest and dividend rates, with reference to the financial plan in the medium and long-term plan and the estimated balance sheet.

(2) Finance-Related Expenses

Like finance-related revenues, interest expenses are calculated based on the expected interest rates with reference to the financial institution lending rates. In the case of long-term debt at a fixed interest rate, the accrued amount is characterized as predetermined. This finance-related expense should be included in an annual budget.

(3) Revenue and Expenses other than Finance-Related
The company must calculate the budget by account in reference to the occurrence of revenue and expenses of the previous years and expectations for the current budget period.

13. Investment/Capital Budget
(1) Equipment Budget
The budget is created by translating the equipment plan in the medium-term and long-term plan into an equipment budget. For large-scale capital investment, the company reflects new equipment purchases in accordance with the equipment plan (which is usually based on sales plan and capacity plan and outsourcing strategy). Since small-scale capital investment may not be incorporated into the equipment plan, the company allocates the required amount adjusted to the actual situation of each department, taking into consideration the trend of previous years.

(2) Investment Budget
Investment budgets are also created in line with financial plan and other related plan in the medium and long-term plan. Most projects already incorporate the investment budget in the medium and long-term plan.

14. Fund Budget
Income and expenditure funds are incorporated into the budget. This is often calculated as a result of the amount of each account in the profit and loss budget (e.g., equipment budget, investment budget, etc.). It is necessary to consider financing/borrowing options to ensure sufficient working capital.

If the large-scale capital investment is planned, the company must determine how to finance the expected expenditure. It can borrow from financial institutions, issue corporate bonds, and utilize direct procurement by a capital increase, otherwise known as capital infusion. It is necessary to consider an optimal business portfolio. In addition, the company must create a capital budget by providing a target value for its financial structure. The company should aim to bring its financial ratios, such as capital adequacy ratio, current ratio and long-term fixed conformity ratio, closer to the predetermined target value. This cornerstone of budgetary control ensures the safety of the company.

> **KEYWORD**
> - **Capital Adequacy Ratio (Equity Ratio)**: an indicator of the proportion of equity capital to total assets. An indicator for company's solvency.
> Capital adequacy ratio (%)
> $$= \text{shareholders' equity (equity capital)} \div \text{total assets} \times 100$$
> - **Current Ratio**: an indicator of the proportion of current assets to current liabilities. The higher the ratio, then the less dependent on short-term capital. Typically 200% is ideal in Japan, anything greater than 100% is usually pretty good.
> Current ratio (%) = current assets ÷ current liabilities × 100
> - **Long-term Fixed Conformity Ratios**: an indicator to what extent fixed assets are covered by shareholders' equity (equity capital) and long-term debt.
> Long-term fixed conformity ratio (%)
> $$= \text{fixed assets} \div (\text{shareholders' equity} + \text{long-term liabilities}) \times 100$$

15. Overall Budget

The overall budget, or company-wide budget, is the integration of all budgets created by all departments. An overall budget helps determine the target forecast of the company as a whole. It reflects the intentions of both the whole company and the people who developed the overall budget. In some cases, the budget may favor some departments, but are unfavorable for the company as whole. The best overall budget must benefit the whole company, not just selected departments. The budgeting department plays a central role in the coordination between management and each department, as well as among every department. The company must thoroughly review whether the measures for eliminating contradictions between the budgets have been incorporated in the budget. Improvement in the accuracy for feasibility and the growth of the company must also be incorporated in the budget.

16. Review of Budget

To achieve the purpose of budget management, the company should review the budget in a timely manner. If the prerequisites of budget setting have changed, comparison with the actual results is irrelevant. The budget should not be modified because the performance did not reach the target. The budget must be controlled in a flexible manner.

17. Progress Management of Budget

Once a budget has been developed, the company must manage the progress of the budget. It should be done after any incidents and in a timely manner. Sometimes, it is too late to get back to the right track after going in a wrong direction. Nevertheless, the company should continue to aim for a higher level of growth and financial results.

(1) Day-To-Day Management

The manager of each department is in charge of day-to-day management. The manager oversees business operations by evaluating the achievements of the subordinates, reviewing their progress reports, and providing guidance and support. Day-to-day management should comply with the rules of the organization, rather than relying only on the ability of the manager. Specifically, company policies and manuals should be in place.

(2) Monthly Management

Monthly management plays a central role of budget control. The monthly management involves analyzing the difference between the budget and actual results. It takes into account the performance data of the previous month and the year-over-year performance data. The management and the head of each department are responsible for these roles. Specifically, they manage the progress of business operations through monthly meetings, individual discussions, etc. The content of the differences determines if improvements in any business operations are necessary. They provide each department with a feedback report and develop measures for improvement.

(3) Semi-Annual Management

Semi-annual, or 6 months, is the right period of time which allows the company to understand the prediction differences of the economic environment. Hence, reviewing the budget is also made easier. If the deviation between the target and the actual results increases, it will be difficult to carry forward the unachieved part over to the second half of the fiscal year. Restoring the company's performance to the original target level will be a challenge. This can severely weaken employee motivation to achieve the company goals. In order to achieve the yearly budget goals, the company must understand the progress of the budget in the middle of the period and take into account the rest of the full year.

(4) Appointment Budget Administrator

Progress management does not work without a budget administrator. It is necessary to appoint an administrator responsible for each budget management unit. The responsible administrator should be granted the authority required to achieve the targets. The budget administrator motivates other managers and their subordinates to achieve the goals. Successfully met targets should be associated with the evaluation of individual employees involved in this achievement. The company's commitment to target management system can be introduced as a way to define the responsibility of individual employees. Additionally, it can be used to enhance their motivation. The following points should be brought to attention to introduce this system. (i) Firstly, the priority of evaluation criteria is given to the goal achievement of individuals. Goal setting becomes second. (ii) Secondly, the managers of the company must set their own goals. They must be committed to achieving said goals and disclose them to the staff members within the organization.

18. Analysis of Variance between Budget and Actual Results

An analysis of variance between budget and actual results is required for budget control. The differences may work advantageously or disadvantageously. The company needs to understand the reasons for the differences. In some cases, the favorable variance may not be caused by the effort of business operations but by an accidental element. If unfavorable and not by accident, countermeasures must be considered to fill the gaps.

Variance analysis helps the company improve business operations. In addition, it also helps in conducting the performance evaluation of the management.

If the budget is not achieved, variance analysis helps clarify who is responsible for the result and associating it to the performance evaluation. If the analysis result shows that there is anything to be achieved for the next year, it should be reflected it in next year's budget. The accounting and finance department should not be "satisfied" with the monthly report of variance analysis between budget and actual results. There are several important things to understand: (1) the current performance; (2) the anticipated result of each quarter (or the first half of the year); (3) the reasons for failed goals, if any; and (4) providing the objective financial data together with the backup data to the highest decision making body for discussion to achieve the target.

[Example of form]
Budget vs. Actual Result

Product name	Sales			Gross profit on sales			Selling general and administrative expenses			Operating profit		
	Budget	Actual	Difference	Budget	Actual	Difference	Budget	Actual	Difference	Budget	Actual	Difference
○○○												
×××												
△△△												
Total												

Reasons for the difference

• Sales

• Selling general and administrative expenses

Roiling Forecast

The regular budget is formulated once a year by spending an enormous amount of time. Since the business environment has changed rapidly in recent years, the developed budget can become obsolete in a very short span of time. Therefore, some companies, mainly foreign-owned companies, have adopted the Rolling Forecast method. It is a forecast approach used to regularly enhance the accuracy of performance forecasts. Companies can control this forecast instead of the normal budget, and are not bound by the budget.

The rolling forecast is usually done on a quarterly basis. It will reflect the information of the current situation more accurately. It has a flexible and

10. Annual Budget Management

advantageous feature that can respond to changes in the business environment. The rolling forecast enables the company to control more continuous business operations, without being bound by the one year period. The accounting and finance departments of foreign-owned companies put priority on forecasts. They have the FP&A function (Financial Planning & Analysis) as a dedicated department.

 Tips for Good Accounting Practices!

- Create the budget by maintaining consistency with the medium and long-term plan. An analysis of variance between budget and actual results helps a lot in management.

11. Cash and Bank Control

Cash and bank accounts might have high risk for fraud and errors due to the nature of the instrument. In order to prevent fraud, such as embezzlement or misappropriation of cash, the company must place appropriate controls over cash and bank accounts handling.

Process Flow

Cash and bank accounts controlling activities can be divided into the following types.
- Bank Deposits and Withdrawals: Controlling deposits and withdrawals utilizing bank accounts.
- Check: (*Cheque* in British English): A written document that instructs a bank to pay the stated amount from the account of the issuer (payer) to the beneficiary (payee) on the document.
- Petty Cash Control: A cash on hand controlling method utilizing the petty cash system.
- Cash and Bank Accounts Control: Controlling balance of cash on hand, bank deposits and cash equivalents.

1. Bank Deposits and Withdrawals
(1) Receiving Fund by Bank Transfer or Bank Deposit

Until recently, since companies had received actual cash and checks from customers in house, they were subject to fraud and errors. Now, due to the development of electronic banking through internet or closed network such as ZenginNet in Japan, FRB system in U.S. or SwiftNet depending on the country, many companies receive payments directly from the suppliers via bank transfer. The accounting/finance department needs to confirm the amount and reason of the credit transactions in the bank accounts and records them appropriately.

11. Cash and Bank Control

> **KEYWORD**
>
> - **Bank Transfers**: The typical type of bank transfers are Wire Transfer and ACH (Automated Clearing House) that moves funds from the payer's account to the payee's account. The fund is available within the same day in the case of Wire Transfer. In the case of ACH, it takes one or two days until the fund becomes available. Bank transfer methods: An internet banking agreement with a bank makes bank transfers through an internet connection terminal possible. This type of electronic fund transfer may use a dedicated communication network or the internet.

【Bank Receipts Verification Flow】

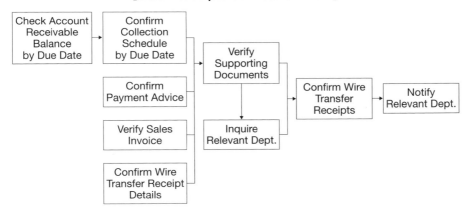

(2) Payment by Bank Transfer

With the exception of countries where checks are still commonly utilized, the majority of companies make payments through bank transfers. Upon receipt of the payment request from the department in charge, accounting/finance department needs to verify the adequacy of the payment, execute the payment based on the request and record it in the accounting book. For electronic payment systems, there is usually a manual or electronic matching of the Purchase Order, Receipt and Invoice (3-way match) before the payment can be completed.

(3) Check (or Cheque) Payment

After the checks are issued by the payer and sent to the payee, they are received and deposited by payee to its bank account. Those checks are then returned to the issuing bank mainly through clearing house operation for verification of the payer's 1) Authorized Signature and 2) Fund Availability. Until the time when both are confirmed by the issuing bank, amount on the checks would not be debited to the payer's bank account. Thus, there usually have some discrepancy in bank account balance between the payer's book and the bank statement since the payer normally debits bank ledger account at the time of the check issuance.

> **KEYWORD**
>
> - **Payment Verification**: Upon the receipt of the Payment Request, Accounting checks with the contents of the supporting documents appropriateness of the payee, amount, timing, method, ledger account and other details and forward for execution.

【Payment Verification Flow】

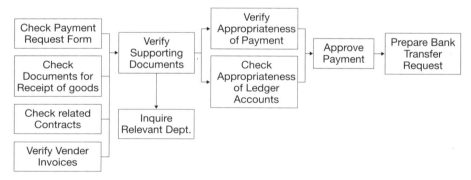

11. Cash and Bank Control

【Payment Execution Flow for Bank Transfer】

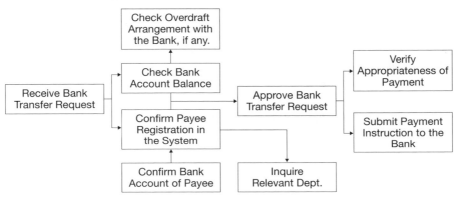

2. Petty Cash Fund Control

Payment procedures are, in principle, performed through the accounting/finance department. As the scale of the company expands, processing all payments through the head office becomes inefficient. In this case, companies may transfer the functions of payment of small expenses, or daily expense needs, to a specific division, department, branch office, or factory. They provide the responsible party with cash in advance that is managed as a petty cash fund.

However, in the recent move of minimizing risk of fraud and strengthen internal control, there are some companies that abolished the petty cash system.

(1) Check Replenishment Request by Accounting/Finance Department

Accounting/finance receives the cash replenishment request and reviews the appropriateness of the expense items. It checks that the petty cash on hand and the amount on the receipts add up to the initially set imprest amount. Then, accounting/finance department Implements the replenishment and records the amount that was actually disbursed from the petty cash in the book of accounts.

(2) Role of the Department which Maintains the Petty Cash Fund

The Petty Cash Fund is maintained on an imprest basis with one individual responsible for the fund, the Petty Cash Fund Custodian. The Petty Cash Fund Custodian of the department submits a Replenishment Summary (summary of expense), attaching the necessary official receipts, sales invoices and other documents as well as the petty cash replenishment requests to accounting/finance. As cash is an easily stealable commodity an appropriate safe should be procured with safeguards as to access along with adequate insurance to cover theft. This extends to collection and depositing cash at banks

【Petty Cash Fund Replenishment Flow】

KEYWORD

- There are two controlling methods in the petty cash systems: **"cash advance system (imprest system)"** and **"supply as needed system."**
- (i) **Imprest System**: The petty cash custodian of each department or branch office is provided a certain amount of petty cash for advance payment. The custodian makes a report about the transactions for a certain period of time using payment reports and other documents and sends it to the accounting and finance department of the head office. The custodian also makes a request for replenishing the amount of money spent so that the person can keep the original amount of cash on hand. In this method, it is easy to check the replenished cash against supporting documents. The reports from the petty cash custodian help reduce the work load of the accounting department of the head office. For these reasons, the imprest system is predominantly adopted and used in practice.
- (ii) **The "Supply as Needed" system**: This method supplies petty cash from time to time according to the needs of each department or branch. In this method, the cash balances held by a petty cash custodian fluctuate constantly and the timings of the reports are irregular. This controlling system is less efficient compared to that of the imprest system.

11. Cash and Bank Control

3. Cash and Deposit Balance Control
(1) Cash Balance Control
When collecting actual cash from its customer, the person in charge should update the Cash Book every day and compare the balance of the actual cash on hand with the balance on the Cash Book. List the actual denomination of cash on hand. If there is a discrepancy, the person in charge must discover its cause as follows: Compare cash book with journal voucher, AR ledger by customer and AP ledger by vender. Compare journal voucher with customer receipts.
Check any cash in and out transactions without having evidences.

【Cash Balance Comparison Flow】

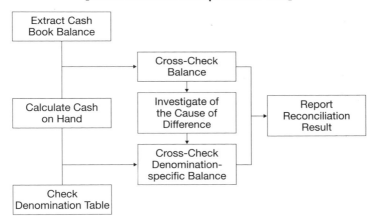

(2) Bank Deposit Balance Management
(i) The person in charge records all the debit and credit transactions in the company bank accounts based on the documents provided by the banks to the Bank Deposit Ledger without any omissions and errors.
(ii) The person in charge needs to create a Bank Reconciliation Report and cross-check balance on the bank statements with Bank Deposit Ledger for each Bank Account and investigate the cause of discrepancies regularly. In addition, at the fiscal year-end, the statement of the accounts balance from each financial institution needs to be obtained.
(iii) The usage of each bank account needs to be checked and the necessity of each account needs to be evaluated regularly. Any unnecessary account needs to be

closed or combined after the consideration of the maintenance cost and relationship with the financial institution.

> **KEYWORD**
>
> - **Bank Reconciliation Report**: In principle, the balance of a bank deposit and the balance on the books of account should be consistent, but it may be inconsistent due to various reasons. Current accounts should be reviewed regularly. The company must obtain a statement of the current account from the bank on a set date and confirm its consistency with the ledger balance of the current account. If there is any discrepancy, it is necessary to investigate the cause of discrepancy and make appropriate corrections. This should be documented in the Bank Reconciliation Report. The four common causes of discrepancy are as follow :
> 1. The bank has recorded the receipt of cash, while the company has not recorded it yet.
>   (Example) Bank has received the fund, but the company has not received any notification from the bank.
> 2. The bank has recorded the disbursement of cash, but the company has not recorded it yet.
>   (Example) The payment was made through automatic withdrawal system, but the company has not received any notification from the bank.
> 3. The bank has not recorded the receipt of cash, while the company has already recorded it.
>   (Example) Deposited after bank hours or remains an uncollected check.
> 4. The bank has not recorded the disbursement of cash, while the company has already recorded it.
>   (Example) Checks which have already been issued but have not been cleared yet or not been deposited yet by the payee.

[Bank Balance Reconciliation Flow]

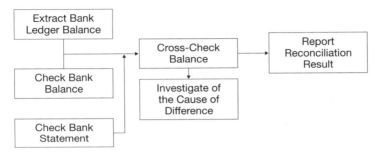

Internal Control Key Points

To design and develop an effective and efficient internal control system for an organization, the company should consider using the COSO's *Internal Control-Integrated Framework* as a guide, an internal control standard broadly accepted internationally. This framework has been often used in regulatory internal control reporting such as for US listed companies in conjunction with Section 404 of the Sarbanes-Oxley Act (SOX) and in Japan for JSOX (the SOX equivalent of Japan).

According to the *Framework*, internal control consists of five integrated components:
- Control Environment
- Risk Assessment
- Control Activities
- Information and Communication
- Monitoring Activities

The following section shall note the considerations for each internal control component.

1. Control Environment
(1) Prohibit Mixing Business and Personal Funds
In small companies, there is a tendency that the cash of the company owner and the cash held by the company may be mixed or managed together. It is necessary to manage business and personal funds separately.

(2) Establish Authority Matrix and Cash Control Policies

The company must define the functional authority and procedures for the person in charge of receipt and disbursement of cash (cashier) by establishing a manual and implementing rules.

2. Risk Assessment
(1) Risk Assessment of Cash Controlling

The following risks are involved in the deposit and withdrawal of cash:
- Cash shortage/excess
- Duplicate payment
- Steal the amount received by forging receipt
- Embezzle cash or deposit
- Process payment of invoices for fictitious transaction in collusion with supplier
- Embezzle by issuing fictitious or unauthorized checks

(2) Mitigate Cash Controlling Risk

(i) Segregation of duties and cross-validation

For internal control purposes, the company should segregate the duties and responsibilities of the approver, the recorder and the custodian of each asset, such as cash.

As a custodian of cash, the cashier should not be engaged in the following operations.
- Payment or payment approval
- Issuance of invoices
- Accounts receivable/accounts payable management
- Recording of Cash Book

(ii) Strict control of receipts

Like Cash Controlling, the company must manage receipts by segregating the duties and responsibilities of the custodian, issuer, and the approver of the official receipt. A cashier or accounting/finance would be responsible for safekeeping unused official receipts. He or she would issue the receipts to the sales department as necessary. The receipts are managed using serial numbers and a ledger is created. It is also necessary to keep cancelled receipts under proper management, rather than discarding them.

In addition, the custodian must affix on the Official Receipt the authorized approver's signature. A signature card with the authorized approver's signature should be provided to major clients to prevent any fraudulent activities.

3. Control Activities
(1) Develop a Manual for Cash Receipts and Disbursements and Enforce Compliance

For the operating procedures that are not included in the regulations, the company must prepare the work manuals and ensure that the work is done in accordance with the manuals.

(2) Rotate Regularly the Person Handling Cash

If the same person is in charge of handling cash for a long period of time, the environment becomes prone to fraud and embezzlement. Therefore, it is highly recommended to regularly replace and rotate the person in charge.

4. Information and Communication

If an incident related to cash occurs, immediate action should be taken to solve the issue. It is also necessary to ensure that a means of communication is available in case of emergency.

5. Monitoring
(1) Compare Cash and Bank Deposit Balance with Ledger Balance and Conduct Cash Count

An employee who isn't in charge of handling the cash should cross-check the actual cash and deposit balance with ledger balance. He or she should conduct a count of cash on a regular basis. This helps in preventing any fraudulent or unauthorized act.

(2) Review Registered Payees (Vendors)

In internet banking and firm banking, registering account information of payees (vendors) is required in advance. It is highly recommended to review the list of registered payees on a regular basis. The company must review inactive payees, delete any unnecessary payees and ensure that the master information is updated. It is important to perform an impromptu review on the list to check whether there are any unknown or doubtful payees.

6. Information and Communication
(1) Recommend Use of Bank Transfer (Wire Transfer, ACH, etc.)

In terms of prevention of fraudulent or unauthorized acts, the best policy is to change payment or collection method from cash or check payment to bank transfer. It also enhances accounting efficiency because the bank transaction records would become readily available.

(2) Safe Keeping of Password for Internet Banking

The increased usage of internet banking has promoted the efficiency of Cash Management activities. On the other hand, there is an inherent risk that the accounting system may be exposed to malicious acts such as phishing and hacking. It is necessary to properly keep passwords and other important information safe, implement appropriate restrictions on user access to the system and accounts, and implement regular and mandatory password changes.

 Tips for Good Accounting Practices!

There are many risks for fraud when handling cash and deposits. Therefore, it is necessary to establish a strict cash controlling system. By keeping cash off company premises, the efficiency of accounting operations is enhanced and the internal control is strengthened.

12. Loan Payable Management

In corporate management, the loan is the most common financing method. The table below is the comparison of typical financing methods: capital increase, corporate bond issuance and loan. A deductible tax on interest expense and a simple procedure characterizes loans.

【Comparison of Features of Capital Increase, Corporate Bond and Loan】

	Repayment obligation	Voting right	Need for collateral	Deductibility of tax on interest	Other features
Capital increase	No	(Shareholders) have voting rights	Not required	No	• It can enhance the ownership equity capital. The credit ratings of a bank can improve due to the increased stability.
Corporate bond	Yes	(Bondholders) have no voting rights	Not required in many cases	Yes	• Most of them are bullet bond.
Bank loan	Yes	(Creditors) have no voting rights	Required in many cases	Yes	• The procedures are easy and quick. • Even during the period of recession, the company can get a loan, if it has a good relationship with the bank. • Installment repayment is common.

Sources: the Ministry of Economy, Trade and Industry "Regional Financial Human Resources Program Textbook"

Banks used to adopt the policy of "collateral guarantee" on real estate and other properties for loan financing (particularly in Japan). After the collapse of the bubble economy in Japan, the examination of financial institutions has been replaced with the policy of "financial statements evaluation". This was made in response to financial policies such as the strengthening of the BIS regulations (see definition in

Keyword for Reference section below), an introduction of prompt corrective action, and a Financial Inspection Manual for financial inspection and self-assessment. Banks review the borrowers on the basis of financial data, focusing on the financial statement. Afterwards, the banks perform a credit rating. Nowadays, these new practices have greatly influenced loan conditions such as interest rates. Thus, the person in charge of loans in the accounting and finance department needs to have the ability to understand the contents of the Financial Inspection Manual, analyze the company's financial data and explain it to financial institutions.

In recent years, Investors Relations (IR) for shareholders has become important for financial institutions. It may also be referred to as the Debt IR. IR refers to all company activities that provide necessary information about investments, like current financial situations, to shareholders and investors. Financial institutions are experts in evaluating the creditworthiness and "stability" of companies. Companies can obtain more favorable loan conditions by disclosing the information required for analysis of the "safety." Companies should also maintain good communication with the financial institutions.

KEYWORD

- **BIS Regulations**: The international unified standards for capital adequacy ratio of banks to do international business. It is also referred to as the Basel agreement. In the BIS regulations, the method of calculating the capital adequacy ratio (only for credit risk of the loan, etc.), minimum standard (8% or more) and the like are established for the G10 countries. Banks that cannot achieve the 8% capital adequacy ratio are forced to virtually withdraw from international operations. In addition to the previous regulations of Basel. Basel II, published in 2004, requires banks to improve the quality of loan. This ensures an appropriate management of loan amount, depending on the creditworthiness of companies including credit rating. Furthermore, although the minimum standards of capital adequacy ratio remains unchanged at 8%, the scope of risks covered is extended to three aspects: credit risk, market risk, and operational risk. In the aftermath of the Lehman Shock, Basel III, published in 2010, requires financial institutions to perform a further review of the quality and quantity of equity capital.
- **Prompt Corrective Action**: In order to prevent the collapse of financial institutions at an early stage and ensure sound management, the financial

12. Loan Payable Management

services agency imposes prompt corrective action on financial institutions which fall below the standard of capital adequacy ratio to improve the business operations. (Japan Financial Service Agency)
- **Financial Inspections**: The Financial Services Agency inspects whether each financial institution carries out self-assessment properly. In principle, financial institutions can finance any company at their own business judgment. By revealing the reality of non-performing loans by inspection, the Agency protects the depositors of financial institutions and stabilizes the financial system. The Financial Inspection Manual guides inspectors in carrying out financial inspection. It was published by the Financial Supervisory Agency (currently the Financial Services Agency) in 1999 and has been revised from time to time. (Japan Financial Service Agency)
- **Self-assessments**: Financial institutions assess and analyze their own assets, such as loans and securities held by the institutions. They classify and categorize the possibility of a loss. An accurate capital adequacy ratio can be calculated because this allows the institutions to prepare proper financial statements by allocating the appropriate depreciation and provision.

1. Types of Loan

Generally, the types of loans of financial institutions are classified as follows:

(1) Loan on Deeds

This type of loan creates a deed, or loan agreement, as evidential documents of the loan. Loan conditions are specified in the deed. Generally, loan on deeds are used for long-term loans for at least a one year period. The purpose of the loan is for real estate, equipment, working capital and many other funds.

(2) Bill of Loan

A borrower draws a bill in favor of a financial institution as documentary evidence of the loan. Due date of the bill is usually a short period of less than one year, such as one month, three months, six months, etc. It is primarily used for working capital. Normally, a "banking transaction contract" is executed between the borrower and the financial institution.

(3) Bill Discount
The commercial bill that a borrower receives in business transactions is discounted and cashed by a financial institution. The payment and discounted bill are settled on the due date of the bill. Normally bills are settled in the period of a month to a few months from the date of drawing. They are used for a short-term working capital source.

(4) Overdraft
The overdraft is a type of loan that sets a credit line based on an "overdraft agreement" with a financial institution. It is then used repeatedly within the credit line. Even if the balance of the checking account becomes negative, the financial institution allows a payment amount to a certain limit. The overdraft makes efficient financing possible and can be an immediate working capital source.

The above four types of loan are the commonly used. Recently, the following loan types are also available

(5) Commitment Line
Commitment line is a credit line that financial institutions have established for the companies which the institution has a business relationship. This system allows the financial institutions to discuss in advance the maximum amount of loan with their client companies. It also provides funds within the credit line to them without any review at any time during a certain period. Enacted in 1999, "The act on Specified Commitment Line Contract" gives financial institutions a greater degree of freedom in setting commitment fees and expanding the commitment line.

The benefits of a commitment line are as follows.
- Companies requiring financing: the company can obtain rapid financing without any review from a financial institution. At the same time, it can streamline its balance sheet by reducing the current liquidity asset.
- Financial institutions: In addition to the normal interest rates, financial institutions can collect contract fees or commitment fees in accordance with the amount of credit line from companies. Thus, the financial institutions can expect a larger fee-based business. The contract of commitment line is performed using the following two methods.

(i) **Bilateral system (relative type)**: a method for concluding an individual commitment line contract with each financial institution.

(ii) **Syndicated system (cooperative type)**: a method for concluding a commitment line contract, under the same conditions, with multiple financial institutions based on a single agreement, with an arranger (as a central coordinating financial institution).

(6) Syndicated Loan (Co Financing)

Syndicated loans are loans for large financing needs made under the same conditions. They are based on a single agreement organized by the syndicate financial group and in cooperation with multiple financial institutions. Specifically, the central coordinating financial institution (a lead bank), as an arranger, sets the interest rates and the period of the loan. They accomplish this by coordinating with the companies involved in capital procurement and sharing financing with multiple financial institutions.

The benefits of syndicated loan are as follows.

- Companies requiring financings without relying on their main bank, the companies can raise large sums of money. The cost efficiency can be enhanced because transaction costs, including the costs of negotiations and office work, are borne by the arranger.
- Financial institutions: While the financial institutions can spread the risk of bad debts, in addition to the lending rate, the central coordinating bank (a lead bank) gains the fee income such as arrangement fees (composition commission) and agent fees. In this way, syndicated loans are characterized by a technique that combines "marketable" as the features of direct financing and "flexibility" as the feature of indirect financing. For this reason, this type of loan is also referred to as a "market-oriented indirect financing".

2. Types of Financial Institutions

City (or Major) banks, regional banks, second regional banks, credit unions, credit association, cooperative associations and government-affiliated financial institutions are financial institutions in Japan that can act as lenders. The features of each financial institution are described below.

(1) City (or Major) Banks

City banks have their branch offices across the country and provide easy access to local customers. The lending policy is generally difficult to finely adjust to the circumstances of individual regions. They sell stereotyped/standardized loan products, especially to small and medium-sized enterprises. For the non-standard products, credit rating is given top priority. The customers must improve their financial rating in order to avail of the city bank's products.

(2) Regional Banks and Second Regional Banks

Regional banks have a particular region as an operating area. They are expected to contribute to the community (relationship banking). For industries and companies that are important in the region, regional banks do not evaluate them solely on their financial reports. They also check the support and assistance that these companies have provided in their region. Therefore, in loan, it is also important to be able to appeal the contribution that may suit the bank.

(3) Credit Unions/Credit Association/Cooperative Associations

These are financial institutions for the purpose of mutual aid of the members and the union members. Said members can expect fine-tuned services. Generally, the loan conditions are not so good as compared to those of the financial institutions mentioned in (1) and (2).

(4) Government-Affiliated Financial Institutions

Government-affiliated financial institutions provide loan services mainly to the fields which private financial institutions have difficulty servicing. In particular, financing programs such as start-up and support turnaround initiatives are also fully established. Lower interest rates and more fixed interests are applied compared to other financial institutions. Therefore, the loan parties may be treated with favorable conditions. On the other hand, they are characterized by poor flexibility of the system, compared to private financial institutions.

Process Flow

Loan payable management work can be divided in two main stages. (1) "Loan Execution" is the stage of reviewing the loan option before the actual loan application. (2) "Outstanding Loan Management" is the stage after the loan is executed.

12. Loan Payable Management

1. Loan Execution

Review Loan Option 〉 Sign Loan Agreement 〉 Execution of Loan

(1) Review Loan Option (Consideration of Loan Conditions)

In loan funds, the applicant must first consider the terms and conditions of the loan (loan conditions or loan requirements). Ideally, he or she needs to determine the following conditions based on the cash flow and cash flow analysis etc.
- Loan amounts: How much to borrow?
- Loan types: Bill of loan, loan on deeds bill discount, or overdraft?
- Loan maturity: When to repay?
- Loan dates: When to borrow?
- Loan interest rates: What percentage the interest rates will be? The rate is usually determined by putting a fixed add-on rate (margin received by financial institution) on market interest rate. The financial institution will still determine add-on amount.
- Repayment method of principal and interest: How many payments will it take to pay off the loan?
- Collateral: what to provide as collateral

【Loan Conditions Verification Flow】

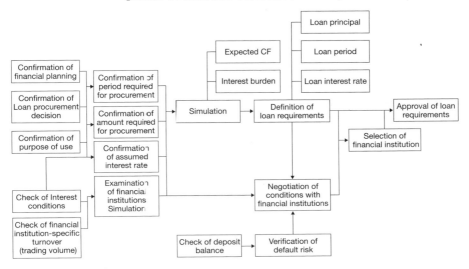

Payment Term and Interest Type

Loan is classified as long-term when the payment term is beyond one year. However, loans with payment terms of less than one year are classified as short-term (Note1). Interest rates are as follows.
- **Long-term variable interest rate**: long-term prime rate + spread
- **Long-term fixed interest rate**: to be determined at the time of loan based on the long-term interest rate: swap rate
- **Short-term interest rate**: shot-term prime rate + spread
- **Short-term interest rate**: market interest rate (LIBOR/TIBOR (Note2)) + spread

In descending order, the interest-rate levels are typically as follows: long-term prime rate, short-term prime rate, and market interest rate. The rate and spread applied changes depending on the power relationship between the borrower and the financial institution. The difference in procurement capacity between financial institutions is also a factor.

(Note1) Long-term and Short-term Loans: In accounting, the long-term loans payable are disclosed on the balance sheet as part of non-current liability if the repayment date exceeds one year from balance sheet date. However, the short-term loans payable are disclosed in the balance sheet as part of current liability if the repayment due date does not exceed one year from balance sheet date.

(Note 2) LIBOR/ TIBO
- **LIBOR** stands for London Inter-Bank Offered Rate. It is used as an international reference for funding costs, and it is an indicator of the procurement cost.
- **TIBOR** stands for Tokyo Inter-Bank Offered Rate.

(2) Sign Loan Agreement

Once the loan conditions are established, the borrower enters into a loan agreement with the lender.

12. Loan Payable Management

(3) Execution of Loan
After signing of the loan agreement, the financial institution transfers the loan proceeds to the company's own account.

2. Loan Management
After borrowing, the company must perform Outstanding Loan Management to process loan repayments.

(1) Loan Interest Management
After borrowing, the company confirms the loan conditions, prepares the loan interest payment schedules and manages the payment. This ensures that no delays on payment occur in accordance with the loan agreement.

Calculation Method of Interest

Calculation method of interest is as follow.
Interest
= [principal] × [interest rate] × [number of days of loan] ÷ 365 days
- **Number of days of loan**: It includes either one end or both ends. **"Including one end"** is the method that excludes either the loan date or the repayment date in the loan days. **"Including both ends"** is the method that includes both the loan date and the repayment in the loan days.
- **Denominator**: It is usually 365 days. If LIBOR applies, it is 360 days. Sometimes this is specifically designated in the loan agreement.

---

(2) Outstanding Loan Management
The company confirms the loan conditions, prepares the loan ledger, and manages the payment according to the loan payment schedule. The loan payment schedule should be in accordance with the loan agreement. At the end of the financial year, it is necessary to obtain statements of accounts from the lender and reconcile the outstanding balance with company's record.

【Loan Ledger Management Flow】

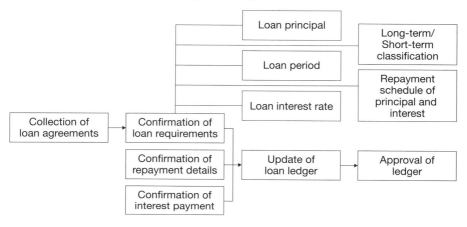

【Balance Verification Flow】

(3) Repayment of Loan

According to the loan agreement, the company needs to confirm the repayment date and the repayment amount. If the collateral has been set, it is also necessary to cancel the registration of the collateral. The repayment method of principals is classified as two types of repayment: (1) Lump Sum Repayment-payment of lump sum on the repayment due date; and (2) Installment Repayment-payment of loan amount in installments over a fixed period of time until the repayment due date. The latter method is further classified as two methods: (a) annuity repayment (equal repayment of principal and interest); and (b) principal equal repayment. The company should consider which method to adopt taking into account the cash flow of the company.

12. Loan Payable Management

[Annuity repayment]
○Features: The principal and the interest are combined to ensure that each repayment amount is the same. The principal will continue to increase in accordance with a decrease of interest.

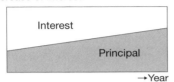

[Principal equal repayment]
○Features: As loan balance decreases the interest also decrease. The principal part is repaid in equal amounts (fixed amount).

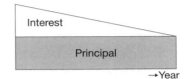

Internal Control Key Points

1. Control Environment

The company should define the authority and procedures of managers and responsible persons pertaining to loans. This is accomplished by establishing functional authority rules and regulations. In the Companies ACT in Japan, "a large amount of debt (loan money, etc.)" requires a resolution of the Board of Directors. The company rules and regulations set the amount criteria that requires a Board of Directors resolution. The company must establish an approval authority, in accordance with the company rules and regulations, for smaller amounts that do not need a Board of Directors resolution. In addition, changing the loan conditions require a prescribed approval from the appropriate authority.

2. Risk Assessment

Risk Assessment for loans are mainly listed below.
(1) Delayed repayment of principal and interest is a risk that can result in interest penalties. In worst case, the company may not be able to borrow in the future due to bad credit reputation.
　　→ Responses: Regularly review the loan ledger to avoid overlooking the repayment date. Thoroughly manage the schedules and other documents.
(2) Variable interest rate is the risk that interest rate will rise in the future.
　　→ Responses: According to regulations or business manuals regarding loan, take any countermeasures to fix variable interest rate, including entering into

an interest rate swap contract. Furthermore, segregate the duties to ensure that interest rates can be routinely watched.

(3) The risk conflicting with covenants.

Financial covenants are loans where the lender requires the borrower to maintain certain financial ratios or a certain amount of cash balance in the bank during the term of the loan.

→ Responses: Establish a procedure to ensure that the person in charge with bank regularly checks that financial ratios or the account balance is sufficient for the financial covenant.

3. Control Activities

(1) Developing Loan Payable Management Manuals and Managing the Application/Compliance.

To establish other rules and regulations including the operating procedures that are not included in the regulations, the company should prepare the work manuals and ensure that the work is done in accordance with the manuals.

(2) Regular rotation of the person in charge.

Management should rotate the person-in-charge on a regular basis by transferring or assigning him to other functions.

4. Information and Communication

The company must ensure that the information on new contracts of loan, contract renewal, and other documents is provided to the accounting and finance department on a regular basis. It must establish a reporting system so that the supervisor can check them.

5. Monitoring

In the workplace, management must thoroughly cross check the loan ledger and the record per book. It should obtain a balance certificate from the lenders on a regular basis and verify the balance.

6. Information Technology

The company is highly encouraged to manage the loan ledger using the software. If possible, use the tools that can automatically calculate interest to avoid any miscalculation. Only the person-in-charge should have access to the software system and his or her supervisor should check on that person regularly. Frequent password changes are also necessary.

Tips for Good Accounting Practices!

- The company must maintain a good communication with financial institutions on a routine basis and disclose any necessary information. Thus the company can raise the required amount of money at a low interest rate in a timely manner.
- It must manage the loan balances using ledgers and other documents to ensure that no delay of the principal and interest repayment of the borrowing occurs.
- Loan transactions with officers or employees of the company are highly discouraged. In fact, these are not allowed in many countries, so confirm any such transactions with the Parent Company.

13. Foreign Exchange (FOREX) Management

If the company has export and import transactions, doing business in foreign currencies will become an integral business process. These transactions are susceptible to exchange rate fluctuations. The management of foreign currency denominated receivables and payables becomes very important because it may affect the bottom-line. If the company manages funds that utilize foreign currency deposits and foreign bonds or if its financing is done in foreign currency, management must consider how to reduce the impact of currency fluctuations.

1. What is Foreign Exchange?

Foreign exchange is the way to settle international transactions involving two parties or more in different countries when there is an exchange of two or more different currencies. This may be done through electronic payment of banks without direct exchange of cash. Foreign exchange enables more cross-border securities transactions. The currency exchange rates of most countries are determined by market force, otherwise known as a floating market. However, there are still countries, like China, which peg their domestic currencies to a major currency such as the U.S.Dollar.

2. Foreign Exchange Market

Banks conduct foreign exchange trading or utilize foreign exchange either pass through the broker or directly between banks commonly referred as interbank market. The interbank market is the wholesale market of the foreign exchange market. Individuals and companies conduct foreign exchange trading at the customer market, more commonly referred to as the retail foreign exchange market.

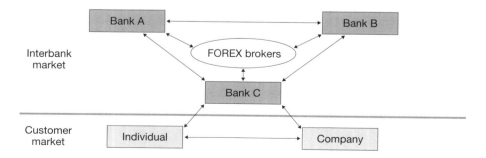

3. Exchange Rate
(1) Interbank Exchange Rate and Customer Exchange Rate
The interbank exchange rate is the exchange rate at the interbank market. The customer exchange rate is the exchange rate at the Retail Foreign Exchange Market. The middle rate (between the bid rate and the offer rate) of the customer exchange rate is derived from the interbank exchange rate. The middle rate is the median average of the selling and buying rate.

(2) Selling Rate and Buying Rate
The Telegraphic Transfer Selling (TTS) is the rate derived by adding one yen to the middle rate representing fees, interest rates, and margins. The Telegraphic Transfer Buying (TTB) is the rate derived by deducting one yen from the middle rate. The terms "selling" and "buying" use the perspective of the bank. If a company buys dollars, TTS will be applied. If it sells dollars TTB will be applied.

(3) Spot Rate and Forward Rate
In the inter-bank market, spot trading uses the value date that comes within two business days from the execution date of the trade contract. The exchange rate applied to the spot trading is called the spot rate. On the other hand, forward trading uses the value date that comes after three business days or more. The exchange rate applied to forward trading is called forward rate. In the Retail Foreign Exchange Market, spot trading generally involves delivery at the time of the conclusion of the contract.

4. Exchange Risk and Hedging Method
(1) Exchange Risk
The exchange risk for companies is classified into the following three types of exposure:
- (i) **Settlement risk** if the company trades with a foreign currency (counterpart currency) instead of its domestic currency (base currency), the risk that the exchange rate may fluctuate during the period of the contract to the settlement is the settlement risk. This fluctuation can affect the cash flow of the company. For example, an exporting company signs a contract in which the payment currency is U.S. Dollar's. However, the Japanese Yen subsequently becomes stronger by the time of settlement. Though the U.S. Dollar's value does not change, the

amount received, when converted to Japanese Yen, will be significantly less. This effectively decreases the export price.

(ii) **Translation risk** if the company's overseas subsidiary keeps its book in currencies other than parent company's domestic currency, an accounting exposure is created if the financial statement has to be consolidated with the latter. After consolidating the financial statements at the end of the fiscal year, the parent company needs to translate the foreign denominated currency accounts into the domestic currency (or functional currency) for statutory reporting purposes. Translation risk occurs at this time. The selection of exchange rate is crucial. Periodic average rate is commonly used for translating income statements of overseas subsidiaries to the domestic currency. Assets and liabilities for each balance sheet presented (including comparatives) are translated at the closing rate at the date of that balance sheet.

(iii) **Economic risk** the risk that involves loss of international competitiveness due to the exchange rate fluctuation is known as economic risk.

(2) Hedging Techniques for Exchange Risk

(i) **Select the same currency for receivables and payables** For instance, a Japanese company uses Yen as its functional currency. It exports in Dollars (receivable are in Dollars) and imports in Yen (payables are in Yen). There is an exposure due to the foreign exchange forward position. When the company changes the currency for exports from Dollar to Yen or the currency for imports from Yen to Dollar, the company's foreign exchange forward position lowers its exposure. This reduces the foreign exchange risk.

> **KEYWORD**
>
> - **Foreign Exchange Forward Positions**: It refers to the difference of a company's foreign currency denominated assets (ex. export accounts receivable, foreign currency deposits) and foreign currency denominated liabilities (ex. import accounts payable, borrowing in foreign currency). If the foreign currency denominated assets exceed the foreign currency denominated liabilities, it is referred to as Long Position. On the other hand, if the foreign currency denominated assets are less than the foreign currency denominated liabilities, it is referred to as Short Position. In addition, the Square or Square Position is the state in which the inflow and the outflow are balanced and perfectly

13. Foreign Exchange (FOREX) Management

> hedged. In the case of Long Position or Short Position, the company is exposed to the risk of exchange rate. It must consider measures to avoid exchange risk in accordance with the company's risk management policy.

(ii) **Financing in foreign currency by exporting companies** In the case of exporting companies, their foreign exchange forward position is likely to be the Long Position. It is possible to reduce the foreign exchange forward position by having a foreign currency loan or by issuing foreign currency bond as financing means.

(iii) **Switching from export to local production** In export, there is a foreign exchange risk in accounts receivables and sales. In local production, such risk is eliminated. However, exchange risk is transferred to the investment accounts of overseas subsidiaries and affiliates. This does not necessarily mean that all foreign exchange risks are completely eliminated.

(iv) **Derivative trading** The company can hedge exchange risk with derivative trading such as forward exchange contracts.

Forward exchange contract refers to a contract of buying and selling a currency on a specific day or during a certain period in the future. For example, the company exports in Dollars and agrees that the money shall be collected in three months. There is a risk that a fluctuation of the FOREX rate may occur in the period of three months and can result in a decreased sales value at the base currency. A forward selling contract makes it possible to determine the base currency value in advance. Thus, forward exchange contract is used as a means to mitigate exchange rate fluctuation risk. Forward exchange contract is made on a negotiation basis.

(v) **Utilize payment netting** Companies which have multiple subsidiaries and affiliated companies operating abroad tend to have several transactions with each other. There is opportunity for reducing the hedging activities and the risk of foreign exchange. For example, the parent company can collectively manage and freely offset receivables and payables between its groups of companies. Thus, only the net amount of foreign exchange transactions requires hedging.

Advantages of Netting

- The company can reduce the occurrence of a loss when the other party goes bankrupt, because the amount of receivables are offset by the amount of payables.

- The company can reduce the exchange commission.
- Funds required for the transaction settlement are reduced, enabling efficient management of funds.
- As compared to the settlement of each transaction, the number of settlements decreases. Less administrative work improves work efficiency.

Classification of Netting

Depending on the number of settlement parties (two parties, or three or more parties), netting can be classified to the following two types:
- **Bilateral nettings**: netting that takes place between two parties. It is intended to offset the settlement between the companies.
- **Multilateral netting**: netting that takes place among three or more parties. It is intended to offset the settlements among the companies within a group or among the companies that are trade partners. With the development of IT, the network systems are constructed more easily. This enables the introduction of multilateral netting.

Process Flow

FOREX Management primarily includes the following tasks:
- **FOREX Management**: development of foreign exchange policy, foreign exchange forward position management, forward exchange contracts management
- **Term-end Evaluations**: evaluation of foreign currency denominated receivables and payables and securities, appropriation of forward exchange contracts and others.
- **Foreign Currency Deposit Management**

1. FOREX Management
(1) Development of Exchange Policy
When executing foreign currency transactions, the first step is to confirm the company's risk management policy. It must develop a policy for hedging foreign exchange risk.

13. Foreign Exchange (FOREX) Management

【Flow of Risk Management Policy Decision-Making】

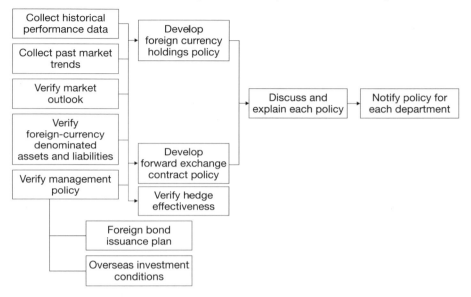

(2) Foreign Exchange Forward Position Management

A. Report on Foreign Exchange Position
The company must know the balances of foreign exchange forward contracts and the foreign currency denominated receivables and payables. Afterwards, it must make a report of the foreign exchange forward position, reflecting the exchange rate fluctuation risk to the management in accordance with the company risk management policy.

B. Ledger Management
The Foreign Exchange Forward Position Ledger must be prepared and updated.

【Flow of Reporting of Foreign Exchange Forward Position】

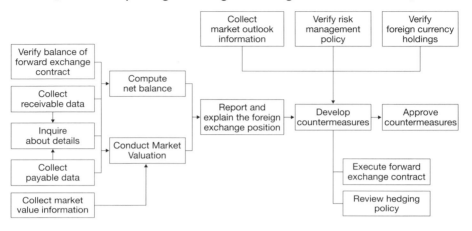

C. Forward Exchange Contracts Management

In accordance with the foreign exchange risk hedging policy of the company, management must obtain predetermined approvals, select suppliers, verify the products, and process the contracts.

The company confirms the transaction requirements, notifies the business partner, exercises its right, and records the transaction in the accounting books after the transaction is completed. The Forward Exchange Contract Ledger manages the previously mentioned transactions.

2. Term-End Evaluation

At the end of the financial reporting term, the company needs to check the foreign currency denominated receivables and payables balances as well as the settlement day rate. Afterwards, it completes the term-end evaluation. If the appropriation of forward exchange contract was conducted, the effectiveness of hedging transactions needs to be confirmed.

13. Foreign Exchange (FOREX) Management

[Valuation and Translation Flow]

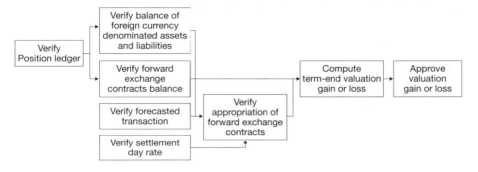

3. Foreign Currency Deposit Management

If the company wants to set the foreign currency deposits, the company needs to prepare and manage a foreign currency deposit ledger. The process is further discussed in Chapter 11 "Cash and Bank Control".

 Tips for Good Accounting Practices!

- The company manages the exchange position balance on a daily basis.
- For accounting purposes, fair market valuation (independent processing) should be used when processing the forward exchange contracts and other derivative transaction. Deferred hedge processing and appropriation processing are possible only if the hedge accounting requirements are accepted.

14. Fund Management

Funds are the blood and lifeline of the company. For a person to be healthy, blood should circulate through all corners of one's body in a sound steady flow. In the same manner, funding is a vital factor for ongoing business activities of the company and for individual departments. Poor cash flow may eventually lead to black-ink (Profitable) bankruptcy, where a company goes bankrupt despite showing a profit on the books. Hence, the Accounting and Finance Departments must monitor its fund flow to avoid shortage of funds and to provide timely funding as needed. Furthermore, all corporate departments should be aware of the importance of fund management.

Process Flow

Fund management mainly involves the following two activities:
- **Medium-term and long-term Fund Management**:
Development of Medium-Term and Long-Term Financial Plans (for a time span of 3-5 years), Performance Monitoring
- **Annual Fund Management**:
Development of an annual (single year) financial plan, Performance Monitoring

1. Medium-Term and Long-Term Fund Management
(1) Development of Medium-Term and Long-Term Financial Plan

The Medium-Term Financial Plan is made based on the Medium-Term Management Plan. In such planning, the funding requirements for 3 to 5 years are estimated based on the Sales Plan, Production Plan, Capital Expenditure Budget (Capital Investment Plan) and Manpower Plan. The company must be able to understand the right side of the balance sheet, or the procurement side of equity and liability. It must also minimize the overall financing costs and review the finance strategy from the viewpoint of ensuring stable funding.

The Medium-Term Financial Plan should focus on the possible provision of equipment and capital investment funds. A Cash Flow Table is commonly used as a supporting document in the Medium-Term Financial Plan.

14. Fund Management

【Medium-Term Financial Plan Preparation Process】

```
Verify repayment schedule ──┐
Verify capital Investment plan ──┤
Verify business income and expenditure ──┼──► Verify fund requirements ──┐
Verify profit plan ──┤    Develop expected capital structure ──┤
Verify interestbearing liabilities balance ──┤                              ├──► Report and explain to management
Verify equity capital ──┤    Develop Financing Plan ──┤
Verify interest rate market trends ──┤    Develop revised interest cost plan ──┘
Collect stock market trends ──┘
```

2. Annual Fund Management
(1) Development of Annual Financial Plan

Like the Medium-Term Plan, the annual budget of the entire company is the basis for the development of the Annual Financial Plan. For short-term planning, fund inflows and outflows should be closely monitored to avoid shortage of funds. The company can prepare a cash budget, an itemized detailed projection of expected cash receipts and disbursements/payments with a beginning cash balance during an accounting period. The Cash Flow Table, Statement of Cash Receipts and Disbursements/Payments, a Sources and Uses Statement and Fund Flow Statements comprise the Annual Budget or Cash Budget.

【Flow of Annual Budget Preparation Process】

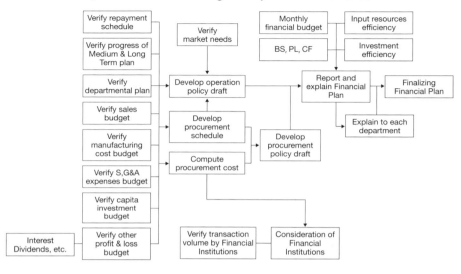

(2) Performance Monitoring

The actual receipts and disbursements/payments are compared and analyzed against the Cash Flow Plan and the Annual Budget on a monthly basis. The results are reported to the management monthly. The Financial Plan shall be revised when necessary. A Cash Flow Table, a Statement of Cash Receipts and Disbursements/Payments, a Sources and Uses Statement and Fund Flow Statements are used as tools for monitoring performance. The Statement of Cash Receipts and Disbursements/Payments is an especially important tool for computing cash positions.

Tips for Good Accounting Practices!

- The profit and loss account does not tally with the account of receipts and disbursements. There should always be a discrepancy (due to non-cash transactions such as depreciation and timing differences between a financial period's activity and receipt and payment of monies).
- Apply a conservative approach in estimating receipts when preparing Statement of Cash Receipts and Disbursement. Figures in an optimistic sales plan should not be relied upon at face value.

Notes

AGS Consulting Co., Ltd., *Practical Manual for Corporate Accounting and Finance* (Tokyo: Chuokeizai-sha Holdings, Inc., 2010)

Akira Kaneko, *Advanced Course in Accounting and Finance* (Tokyo: Nikkei Publishing Inc., 2008)

Akira Kaneko, NTT BUSINESS ASSOCIE Corporation, *Basic Textbook for Corporate Accounting and Finance 3rd edition* (Tokyo: Zeimu Kenkyukai, 2009)

Akira Kaneko, NTT BUSINESS ASSOCIE Corporation, *Basic Textbook for Corporate Accounting and Finance II Step Up Edition* (Tokyo: Zeimu Kenkyukai, 2009)

Akira Kaneko, *CFO Professional I–VI* (Tokyo: JACFO and Kinzai Institute for Financial Affairs,Inc., 2008)

Akira Kaneko, Susumu Nakazawa, Tadashi Ishida, *Comprehensive Income Management* (Tokyo: Nikkei Business Publications, Inc., 2010)

Akira Kaneko, *Globally Accepted, Extremely Easy Japanese-Style Financial Accounting* (Tokyo: Zeimu Keiri Kyokai Co., Ltd., 2011)

Akira Kaneko, *Globally Accepted, Extremely Easy Japanese-Style Management Accounting* (Tokyo: Zeimu Keiri Kyokai Co., Ltd., 2011)

Akira Kaneko, *Business Seminar: Introduction to Corporate Accounting and Finance* (Tokyo: Nikkei Publishing Inc., 2011)

BDO Toyo & Co., *Practical Handbook for Internal Management 4th edition* (Tokyo: Chuokeizai-sha Holdings, Inc., 2009)

CS Accounting CO., LTD., *Basic Textbook for Corporate Accounting and Finance* (Tokyo: Zeimu Keiri Kyokai Co., Ltd., 2010)

CS Accounting CO., LTD., *FASS Examination Textbook and Workbook 2nd edition* (Tokyo: JMA Management Center Inc., 2010)

Deloitte Touche Tohmatsu LLC, *Accounting Process Handbook 5th edition* (Tokyo: Chuokeizai-sha Holdings, Inc., 2009)

Gyosei & CO., *Practical Dictionary of Corporate Accounting* (Tokyo: Nippon Jitsugyo Publishing Co., Ltd., 2009)

JACFO, *Official Guidebook for FASS Examination 2011edition* (Tokyo: JACFO, 2011)

Yusei Audit & Co., *Manual for Developing Accounting Rule* (Tokyo: Zeimu Kenkyukai, 2010)

Notes

Kazuaki Shimazu, Yosuke Higuchi, Kenichi Mieno, *Introduction to Accounting: Accounting Tasks and Preparation* (Tokyo: Subarusya Corporation, 2011)

Koichi Kakutani, *Cost Accounting Glossary* (Tokyo: Dobunkan Shuppan.Co.,Ltd., 1997)

Masaaki Watanabe, *Compendium of Corporate Accounting and Finance* (Tokyo: Nippon Jitsugyo Publishing Co., Ltd., 1998)

Seno Tezuka, *Audit Know-how for Finding the Risk of Material Misstatement 3rd edition* (Tokyo: Chuokeizai-sha Holdings, Inc., 2010)

Yutaka Suzuki, *Understand Accounting Operation with Flowchart* (Tokyo: Chuokeizai-sha Holdings, Inc., 1996)

Ministry of Economy, Trade and Industry, 2003. "Finance and Accounting Service Skill Standard" [Online]
Available at:
http://www.meti.go.jp/policy/servicepolicy/contents/management_support/files/keiri-zaimu.html

About the Authors

Akira Kaneko (1936-2013), Economic Reviewer, Finance Reviewer, and Management Reviewer, was a former CFO to Shin-Etsu Chemical Co., Ltd. and the Senior Advisor to the Japan Association for CFOs.

His major writings, which run to over 130 books, include *Mr. Chihiro Kanagawa: The Management of The World's Best Business Leader* (Second and English Edition / Zeimu Keiri Kyokai Co., Ltd), *How Can-do Presidents Use Money* (English Edition / Zeimu Keiri Kyokai Co., Ltd), *Business Seminar: Introduction to Corporate Accounting and Finance* (Nikkei Publishing Inc.), and *Globally Accepted, Extremely Easy Japanese-Style Financial Accounting* (Zeimu Keiri Kyokai Co., Ltd.).

Tadashi Ishida, CPA, is the Senior Research Fellow (Japan Association for CFOs) and Audit & Supervisory Board Member (Calbee, Inc.). He engaged in audit under J-GAAP/US GAAP and financial advisory services for 25 years from 1972 as a partner with Arthur Young & Co (now Ernst & Young) and Asahi & Co. (now KPMG AZSA). During his tenure at Arthur Young, he worked at its Singapore and London Offices for a total of 10 years. Since 1996, he has held leadership positions as Executive Vice President and CFO of McDonald's Company (Japan) (from 1996 to 2005), Senior Managing Director and CFO of Sega Sammy Holdings Inc. (from 2005 to 2008), and Audit & Supervisory Board Member of Calbee, Inc. (from 2011 to present).

He is a co-author or editor of *Management in the Era of Comprehensive Income* (published by Nikkei BP), *How to Read IFRS Financial Statements* (published by Chuokeizai-sha), and *Accounting & Finance Procedures Manual* (published by Zeimu Keiri Kyokai) (Japanese version only). He is a frequent speaker at seminars and conferences including the IFRS Forum organized by Nikkei BP.

Ryuji Aoyama, LL.M, CPTA, CIA, is a financial and tax consultant. He has been supporting a lot of financial and tax projects for mainly foreign-affiliated companies as a professional consultant at Resources Global Professionals(RGP) Japan after employed by Nippon Life Insurance Company, PricewaterhouseCoopers Japan, etc. He has published 4 books in the financial and tax area. He has also written some articles as a member of Japan Tax Accounting Academy under Tokyo Federation of Certified Public Tax Accountant's Association.

About the Authors

Kazunori Baba, LL.M, CPTA, is a representative of his tax accounting office in Tokyo.
He set up his tax accounting office in 2007 after the employment by Sumitomo Corp., Urban Renaissance Agency, Shinso Tax Accountant Corp. and etc.
He has also experience as a tax consultant at Tokyo Chamber of Commerce and Industry and Taxpayer Support Center under Shibuya Branch of Tokyo Federation of Certified Tax Accountant's Association.
He has published 6 books in the financial and tax area.

Shinsuke Okuaki, CPA, CPTA, is a representative of his accounting office in Tokyo. He passed CPA (Japan) examination at the age of 22 and got engaged in the audit for some of listed companies at a Big 4 firm and moved to a small but top-notch audit firm after studying in London. He has been managing his accounting office since 2008.
He has taught accounting at Waseda University as a lecturer and published 3 books in the financial and tax area.

Miwako Noda, CPTA, is a representative of her tax accounting office in Tokyo. She was previously employed by Sumitomo Marine and Fire Insurance Company, Limited (Currently Mitsui Sumitomo Insurance Co., Ltd.), Shinso Tax Accountant Corp. and etc.
She has been supporting the accounting and tax returns for mainly newly established companies. She is a lecturer for Kanda University of International Studies and published 2 books and supervised 1 book in the financial and tax area.

Index

[A~C]

Acceptance standard/goods receipt 16
Account scrutiny 65
Accounts payable 14
Accounts receivable 1
Accounts Receivable Ledgers 3
Accrual concept 56
ACH 89
Actual Cost Computations 47
Aggregate Billing/Invoicing 5
Aging 6
Aging Test 6
Allowance method 10
Annuity repayment 108
Audit Findings 67
Audit Report 67
Bad Debt(s) 8, 10
Bank Reconciliation Report 93, 94
Bank Transfers 89
Bilateral nettings 116
Bill Discount 102
Bill of Loan 101
Bin Card 26
BIS Regulations 100
Bottom-up method 76
Budget 72
Capacity Utilization 81

Capital Adequacy Ratio (Equity Ratio) 83
Capital expenditure 39
Cash Advance 52
Cash Book 93
Check 88
City (or Major) Banks 103
Closing adjustments 63
Closing Analysis 66
Closing policy 60
Closing schedule 61
Commitment Line 102
Common expenses 62
Compromise method 76
Consumption Basis 20
Contents 43
Cooperative Associations 104
Cost 47
Cost Budgeting 47
Cost of inventories 31
Cost of Sales Budget 78
Cost Variance Analysis 47
Credit Association 104
Credit Investigation 3
Credit Limit 3
Credit Management 1
Credit Unions 104
Current Ratio 83
Customer exchange rate 113

Index

[D~F]

Debt IR 100
Deferred and accrued accounts 63
Delinquent Receivables 6
Depreciable assets 43
Depreciation 40, 44
Direct write-off method 9, 10
Disposal 40, 44
Drop ship 20
Economic risk 114
Employee Master File 52
Equipment Budget 82
Exchange risk 113
Expense 51
Financial Closing 60
Financial Inspections 101
First-in, First-out Method (FIFO) 33
Fixed Asset Ledger 39
Fixed costs 80
Foreign exchange 112
Foreign Exchange Forward Positions
 114
Forward exchange contract 115
Forward rate 113
Fund Budget 82
Funds 120

[G~I]

General Administrative Expenses
 Budget 81
Government-Affiliated Financial
 Institutions 104
Impairment 40
Imprest System 92
Indirect expenses 62
Individual Billing/Invoicing 5
Inspection Basis 20
Inspection standard 16
Intangible fixed asset 37

Interbank exchange rate 113
Inventory 24
Inventory Index Card 26
Inventory period 29
Inventory Tag 26
Inventory Turnover Ratio 30
Investment Budget 82
Investment/Capital Budget 82
Investments and other assets 37
Investors Relations (IR) 100

[J~L]

Labor Cost Budget 79
Last-in, First-out Method (LIFO) 33
LIBOR 106
Loan 99
Loan ledger 107
Loan on Deeds 101
Long-term Fixed Conformity
 Ratios 83

[M~O]

Manufacturing Cost Budget 80
Margin Settlement 52
Material Cost Budget 79
Monthly closing 55
Monthly Performance Management
 55
Multilateral netting 116
Netting 115
Non depreciable assets 43
Non-Operating Profit and Loss Budget
 81
One Year Rule
 (Accounting Period) 64
Operating Cycle Criteria 64
Overall Budget 83
Overdraft 102

[P~R]

Payment Verification 90
Payroll 52
Periodic average rate 114
Periodic Inventory System 27
Perpetual Inventory System 27
Petty Cash 88
Physical Inventory 24
Policy on Payment 14
Policy on Supplier selection 14
Principal equal repayment 108
Production Budget 79
Prompt Corrective Action 100
Proper inventory level 28
Purchase Discount 18
Purchase Rebate 18
Purchase Returns and Allowances
.... 18
Rebates 7
Receipt Basis 20
Regional Banks 104
Repair 39
Replenishment Summary 92
Retail Method 33
Roiling Forecast 86

[S~U]

Sales Allowance 7
Sales Budget 78
Sales Discount 7

Second Regional Banks 104
Segregation of Duties 22, 53
Self-assessments 101
Selling Expense Budget 79
Settlement risk 113
Software 43
Specific Identification Method 33
Spot rate 113
Standard Cost Method 33
Subsequent Events 66
Suppliers Warehouse 20
Supply as Needed 92
Suspense accounts 63
Syndicated Loan (Co Financing) 103
Tangible fixed asset 37
Tax Effect 65
Telegraphic Transfer Buying (TTB)
.... 113
Telegraphic Transfer Selling (TTS)
.... 113
Terms and Conditions 3
TIBOR 106
Top-down method 75
Translation risk 114

[V~Z]

Variable costs 80
Version upgrade 44
Weighted Average Method 33
Wire Transfer 89

Introduction to Japanese "Accounting and Finance" Practices

2017年12月20日　初版発行
2025年5月20日　初版第2刷発行

監修者	金児　昭
編著者	石田　正
著　者	青山隆治
	馬場一徳
	奥秋慎祐
	野田美和子
発行者	大坪克行
発行所	株式会社 税務経理協会

〒161-0033東京都新宿区下落合1丁目1番3号
http://www.zeikei.co.jp
03-6304-0505

整版所	株式会社森の印刷屋
印刷所	株式会社技秀堂
製本所	牧製本印刷株式会社

本書についての
ご意見・ご感想はコチラ

http://www.zeikei.co.jp/contact/

本書の無断複製は著作権法上の例外を除き禁じられています。複製される場合は，そのつど事前に，出版者著作権管理機構（電話03-5244-5088，FAX03-5244-5089, e-mail: info@jcopy.or.jp）の許諾を得てください。

JCOPY ＜出版者著作権管理機構　委託出版物＞
ISBN 978-4-419-06503-4　C3034

© 金児昭・石田正・青山隆治・馬場一徳・奥秋慎祐・野田美和子 2017 Printed in Japan